D0096449

GHOST INVESTIGATOR

Volume I:
Hauntings of the Hudson Valley

To Michael, Boo! 10/29/03

Written by
Linda Zimmermann

A
Spirited
Books
Publication

Also by Linda Zimmermann

Bad Astronomy
Forging A Nation
Civil War Memories
Ghosts of Rockland County
Haunted Hudson Valley
More Haunted Hudson Valley
Haunted Hudson Valley III
A Funny Thing Happened on the Way to Gettysburg
Rockland County: Century of History
Mind Over Matter
Home Run
Ghost Investigator, Volume 2: From Gettysburg, PA to Lizzie Borden, AX

The author is always looking for new ghost stories. If you would like to share a haunting experience go to:

www.ghostinvestigator.com

Or write to:

Linda Zimmermann
P.O. Box 192
Blooming Grove, NY 10914

Or send email to:
lindazim@frontiernet.net

Cover Art by Gordon Bond: tpoastro@hotmail.com

Ghost Investigator
Volume I: Hauntings of the Hudson Valley
Copyright © 2002 Linda Zimmermann

All rights reserved. This book may not be reproduced in whole or in part without permission.

ISBN: 0-9712326-0-1

Table of Contents

The Birth of a Ghost Investigator

No, this isn't what I went to school for, and it isn't anything I ever planned on doing. So how did I get to be the Ghost Investigator?

When I was a kid I was always fascinated by ghost stories and the paranormal. I remember one story in particular that sent chills up my spine—coffins in a crypt kept rearranging themselves every night until an unwanted family member was removed. To me, it was unthinkable that someone would ever be crazy enough to go inside a place like that, or any other haunted location for that matter. Now, crawling around a basement filled with ghosts is just another day at the office.

My first career was as a research chemist for a diagnostic company. I loved the lab and all its gadgets and instruments, and I certainly got plenty of experience conducting experiments and examining things objectively. However, under that white lab coat beat the heart of writer, and my creative impulses were not to be denied.

I left the lab and started writing about science, history and science fiction. I also found that lecturing about my favorite subjects was just as much fun as writing about them. So, bit by bit, I pieced together a new career, but little did I know that more changes were to come.

In 1997, I was giving a series of lectures in Rockland County, New York, about local history and legends as part of the county's bicentennial events. I got a call from one of the libraries where I was scheduled to speak, and the librarian asked if I knew any local ghost stories to add to my history presentation. I knew only one, and when I told it, I thought that would be the end of it.

About a week later, I got a call from another library. The librarian excitedly said, "I hear you give ghost talks. Could you give one here?" I explained that I was giving history lectures, but decided I had better start gathering more ghost stories to tell. It's a good thing I did, because over the course of the lecture series fewer people attended for the history, while the number of ghost enthusiasts swelled. Then people started calling and asking if I was the "Ghost Lady" they had heard about, and when was I going to publish a book of stories? Opportunity was knocking, as loudly as a spirit rapping on a medium's table.

Initially, I read up on the popular ghost stories that had been passed down from generation to generation. I also interviewed people who had personal stories of hauntings, and occasionally was lucky enough to actually visit a site. My only equipment was a camera and a tape recorder, and I simply gathered eyewitness reports and took some pictures. At first I didn't think I would find enough stories to fill a book, but by the time I completed *Ghosts of Rockland County* in 1998, there were enough additional stories and leads to begin *Haunted Hudson Valley*.

As the short run of *Ghosts of Rockland County* was coming off the presses, I couldn't help but have a queasy feeling in the pit of my stomach. Would people actually buy a book of local ghost stories? Within in short time I had my answer—the entire first edition sold out in two weeks, and I was swamped with offers to give lectures.

All the ingredients for the creation of the Ghost Investigator were now in place. I had a background in both science and writing. My books and lectures fueled interest and brought me in contact with people who had more stories for more books and lectures, etc., etc...

The only things missing were the tools of the trade. If I was in a haunted house and walked into a cold spot, I wanted a way to instantly measure the temperature and see if there were any electromagnetic fields present. I wanted to be able to see in total darkness and record images in infrared. It wasn't enough to say I felt or sensed something—I needed solid data to try to substantiate that something real and measurable was taking place.

So, for Christmas of 1998, I asked my boyfriend to get me an electromagnetic field meter. (Shopping for presents for me is rarely a case of sizes and colors—it is more likely megahertz and horsepower.) Then I bought an infrared non-contact thermometer, a camcorder that tapes in infrared, motion detectors—anything (that I could afford!) that I thought might help put ghost hunting on a firmer scientific foundation.

However, as much as I try to conduct sound, rational investigations, I haven't forgotten a crucial element—telling a good story. Just because I can't stick a meter into something doesn't mean I will disregard it. Part of me is still that kid with a flashlight reading ghost stories under the covers. While I never make up any part of the stories I personally investigate, I realize that not all second-hand sources may be accurate in every detail. What is important in those cases is that the witnesses were credible, the stories were consistent, and when you read them a chill goes up your spine.

Do I have a clue where all of this will take me? No, but that's part of the fun of life. I will keep doing what I do and just see where it all leads. Of course, I would love to be able to someday say, "Here is incontrovertible scientific evidence on the existence of ghosts. This is exactly what they are, and how you can detect, measure and communicate with them."

Until that day comes, I'll keep sticking my meters into dark corners, and at the end of the day pull the cobwebs out of my hair and just tell a good story about it all.

What is a Ghost?

The number one question I am asked is, "What is a ghost?" I believe that the short answer is that it is the spirit of an unhappy or confused dead person. Obviously, it is much more involved than that, and volumes have been written trying to explain the intricacies of the human soul and its journey after death.

Of course, if you are living and breathing you are not completely qualified to discuss what happens on the other side, but intuition and experience can allow you to hazard a guess. So here is my unofficial opinion:

First of all, you have to believe that there is more to life than merely a physical body. There must be a spirit or soul, or none of this makes any sense. Personally, I can't understand how anyone could withstand the blatant unfairness and cruelties of life if they didn't appreciate the fact that the world is a school for the soul. You may not like the lessons, but you have to learn them either sooner or later. (Trust me, make it sooner or it could be a lot later.)

The next ingredient in creating a ghost is death. The physical body must be shed so that the spirit is released. Now I know many people have reported out-of-body experiences when they are alive, but the spirit is still tethered to the body, and will remain so, until death severs that tie.

The next question would be why some spirits cling to their old houses, or places where they died, etc. This is the key ingredient, the thing that separates the ghosts from the "free spirits," and the only part of this equation over which we have any real control. If you were born, you are going to die; that's not an option. Where you have control is over what happens in between. That's the part we call life.

Are you living a life without any regrets? Have your words or actions never harmed another person? Are you always doing the right thing? Are you completely unattached to your possessions?

If you answered yes to all of these questions you are obviously a saint and don't need to worry. However, if you are human like the rest of us, there is the potential to get stuck between worlds when you die.

If you look for common threads in causes of hauntings, you invariably find suicides, anger, hatred, grief, regret and guilt. It is the people who cannot let go of the strong negative emotions that seem to be doomed to repeat their behavior after death. In the case of murder victims, I think the shock and anger often compels their spirits to remain to seek vengeance and sympathy, when what they really need to do is move on and let the matter be resolved in a higher court.

Many people have told me there's no problem with the ghost in their house because it's just a former owner who doesn't want to leave. They feel their ghost is happy and there's no need for concern. Let me state again, there is no such thing as a happy ghost. Confused, yes. Happy, no.

It's like you have spent your entire life preparing for a big trip, you finally get to the airport and then forget that you are supposed to get on a plane. You may think that hanging out in the terminal for all of eternity is fun, but I would prefer to get where I'm going.

I would also like to make a definite distinction between encountering a ghost attached to this world, and communicating with the spirit of a friend or loved one. While the experience could be similar, a ghost is confined to a particular location and has a particular agenda. To use the airport analogy again, it's the difference between the happy world traveler who may send a postcard whenever he feels like it, and the passenger going nowhere in the terminal, repeating the same story over and over.

My advice? Live the best life you can. If you know something is wrong or harmful, don't do it. If you have a dream, follow it. And most importantly, never underestimate the power of joy and compassion, and the benefits of happiness.

Okay, I'm finished with "Life and Death 101." Enjoy the stories.

About This Book

This is a collected work of four previously published books, *Ghosts of Rockland County*, *Haunted Hudson Valley*, *More Haunted Hudson Valley*, and *Haunted Hudson Valley III*. Rather than continue to reprint four small books, I decided to update the stories, combine them into a single volume and launch the *Ghost Investigator* series.

Please note that out of respect for the privacy of individuals and their property, some names have been changed and only approximate locations are mentioned. Those names that have been changed are introduced in quotation marks.

For other places such as parks, restaurants and cemeteries, I would encourage you to visit them—respectfully, of course.

If you have any questions or comments about the material contained in these stories, or know of a site to investigate, contact me at:

Linda Zimmermann
P.O. Box 192
Blooming Grove, NY 10914

Or at:

www.ghostinvestigator.com

To the potential ghost in every person:

Take care of your own problems now,
so others aren't haunted by them later.

Book One

THE ANGRY POLTERGEIST

The term poltergeist is a composite of two German words, which literally mean "create a disturbance" and "ghost." While you might consider any disembodied spirit of the dead roaming around your house to be a disturbance, some ghosts are clearly far more disturbing than others. Cold spots, shadowy forms and wailing cries in the dead of night are definitely unnerving, but the ghosts associated with these experiences are often benign and pose no immediate threat to the living. Poltergeists are another story. Their behavior runs the gamut from annoyingly mischievous to frighteningly dangerous. For example, what would you do if unseen hands started throwing heavy objects at your head? What if your particular haunting involved a poltergeist, a very angry poltergeist?

In the boom years after World War II, Rockland County, New York saw a spurt in growth as many veterans and their families looked for a peaceful alternative to the hustle and bustle of New York City. Famous people from the world of the arts and entertainment also chose to make the sleepy little county their home. One such man was Danton Walker, a columnist, who upon moving to his 18th century home on Quaker Lane in Mt. Ivy, unfortunately found no peace and little sleep.

The first disturbance Mr. Walker encountered was someone loudly and persistently banging the heavy knocker on his front door. When he went to investigate, he would find no one there. Assuming it was a prankster, he thought to foil the miscreant by installing a screen door in front of the wooden door. After the screen door was in place, he locked it securely, making it impossible to reach the knocker. Walker was confident he had put up the perfect barrier against the mischievous hands. In fact, it was the perfect barrier against human hands, but whatever continued banging the knocker that night as if there was no screen door was obviously not human.

Then even more bizarre things began happening. Mr. Walker was a collector of early pewter pieces, which fit in very nicely with the colonial architecture. Apparently, however, not everyone appreciated the pewter, as one night a piece came off the shelf by itself. This is not to say it slipped off the shelf and fell straight down, it was literally thrown across the room

and landed against the far wall. No living soul had been anywhere near the shelf at the time.

Pewter pitchers and sauceboats then regularly left the shelves and traveled around the room, self-propelled. One particularly expensive pitcher that took flight had been flawless when Walker purchased it. When he picked it up to return it to its shelf, he noticed five indentations. These indentations matched exactly with the pattern of human fingertips, as if someone had gripped the pitcher with inhuman strength. Chances are, it was inhuman.

As disturbing as these events were, Walker tried to cope with the unpleasant situation, until one evening when he was having a party. Once again, a heavy piece of pewter left its resting place on its own, and the unseen hands violently hurled the piece at one of Walker's guests, narrowly missing her head. That was the last straw—the poltergeist had crossed the line from being simply aggravating to being dangerous. Walker decided to take action before anyone was seriously hurt.

Walker contacted Hans Holzer, world famous ghost hunter and author of dozens of books about hauntings (many of which this author used to read under the covers with a flashlight!). Holzer agreed to visit the house and bring along a female psychic with whom he had often worked. They arranged a séance and Danton Walker prepared himself to confront the spirit that had been tormenting him. However, torment took on a new meaning when the sad story of the angry poltergeist came to light.

During the séance, the psychic claimed to have contacted the spirit of a Polish mercenary who had been paid to fight for the British during the Revolutionary War. The mercenary was in the Mt. Ivy area when either British troops mistakenly thought he was fighting for the Americans, or had some other grudge against the Polish soldier. In any event, the British took off after him, and he started to run for his life. The mercenary came upon the house on Quaker Lane, banged on the door, and when no one answered, forced his way inside and tried to hide. The British troops found him and brutally beat him. He was left for dead, but the mercenary was not to be so fortunate as to die quickly.

When he regained consciousness, he found that his leg had been shattered and his skull severely fractured. Unable to move, he suffered the torment of excruciating pain throughout his body. Days of agony passed, and no one came to help. There wasn't even a pitcher of water within reach to quench his terrible thirst. Finally, mercifully, he died several days later.

In the weeks and months following the séance, the pewter remained on the shelves and the nightly banging on the door ceased. Did the tortured spirit of the mercenary finally find release by having the truth of his terrible ordeal become known? Or did he merely lose interest in harassing Danton Walker? Perhaps the poltergeist is still in the house, waiting to vent his anger upon another unsuspecting owner…

2AM WAKE-UP CALL

When one thinks of scary things, high ranch houses usually don't make the list (unless you are a connoisseur of architecture) and they aren't considered to be prime haunting territory. In the ghostly realm, hauntings are popularly associated with shadowy Victorian homes, or old, overgrown colonials with centuries of history. However, this is a misconception. Hauntings can occur anywhere, at any time in just about any way imaginable—and that includes brand new houses in the suburbs.

The hundreds of high ranches that have sprung up across the Rockland landscape in the last generation generally do not draw one's attention, due to their uniformity and sheer number. However, there is at least one of these homes in the county that makes you sit up and take notice, especially at 2 o'clock in the morning.

When the "Guinness" family moved into their new home in Spring Valley in the 1970s, they thought the most frightening things they would have to deal with were the mortgage payments and taxes. Their high ranch was on a quiet cul-de-sac in a relatively new development, so they did not anticipate any problems with the house, and the neighbors all seemed friendly. Once the chaos and confusion of the move had settled down, it seemed as if they would simply get on with the routine life of a suburban family. What they could not have planned for interfering with their lives was something that was quite dead.

One night when the family was sleeping peacefully, the Guinnesses and their children were suddenly awakened at precisely 2am. They were startled, as if something terrible had just happened. However, they were surprised to find that there were no sirens or loud sounds, no flashing lights from a police car or ambulance, and no sharp odors of smoke in the air. In fact, there was nothing out of the ordinary except they were all awake in the dead of night. The house was dark and quiet, and not even a dog could be heard barking in the neighborhood. There was simply no external reason for the entire family to have been roused from their beds at the same time.

The family members did sense something, however, but it was most definitely internal. It was fear; a fear that something, or someone, was in the house. Mr. Guinness jumped out of bed and started down the hall to check on the children's safety, but he had not gone more than a few steps when an icy gust of wind blew past him, or more accurately, through him. Shaking it off, he proceeded to check on the children and found that they were scared, but unhurt. A check of the rest of the house uncovered no intruders, and all the doors and windows were safely secured.

The following night they all awoke with a start again, exactly at 2am. Again, there was a deathly cold blast that swept down the hall. There were no sounds, no lights, only fear. Within days of these inexplicable and unnerving wake-up calls, appliances, radios and televisions started turning on by themselves when no one was in the room. These bizarre occurrences persisted until one night Mr. Guinness shouted out, "I don't care who you are, or what you are doing here, just stop frightening my children!"

Did the outburst have any effect? Things did quiet down enough for the family to manage to live with it for several years, but the unwelcome visitor still made its presence known on a regular basis. The Guinness family finally moved out of the high ranch on that deceptively quiet cul-de-sac, and they were happy to not take everything from the place with them.

There are rumors in the neighborhood about the land upon which the development was built, rumors that something terrible had happened on the spot of the haunted high ranch. The Ku Klux Klan had been active in the area for several decades, holding rallies and burning crosses to intimidate "undesirables." Some of the rumors say that one night the Klan went too far and murdered at least one innocent victim on the land that eventually became the site of the new housing development. As so often happens in such cases, nothing has been proven, but to the Guinness family, they had all the terrifying proof they needed.

Do blenders and televisions still turn themselves on in that innocent looking high ranch in Spring Valley? Does the icy presence still rush down the hall every night at 2am? The Guinness family didn't wait around to find out, but you can't blame them, they have a lot of sleep to catch up on.

A CHILLING TRAGEDY

There is a stately mansion in Tomkins Cove that has been lovingly restored to its original 1850s splendor. Today if you were to walk its serene grounds and see the sunlight sparkling on the river below, it would be difficult to imagine the house as anything but a place of light, warmth and happiness. To the current owners it is such a place and, in fact, generations have led contented lives there. Yet, there may also be something discontented there, something cold and dark trapped by tragic events within the towering walls.

When new owners moved into the magnificent mansion in the early 1990s, the interior was in desperate need of renovation. Ornate plaster ceilings and finely carved wood doorframes needed to be rescued from beneath a century's worth of old paint. The decorative ceiling on the third floor was in danger of collapsing, and in order to save it, scaffolding had to be erected and the entire ceiling had to be raised seven inches so that new supports could replace the rotted beams. Restoration was an enormous task that required many craftsmen and careful attention to detail. The progress was closely watched, perhaps by more eyes than they anticipated.

The first sign of anything unusual came soon after the "Wilson" family had moved in. They were living in a few rooms on the ground floor while the workmen filled the air with plaster dust and the sound of power tools throughout the rest of the house. One night after the workmen had all gone home, and bad weather had prevented Mr. Wilson from making it home, Mrs. Wilson was left all alone. Stretching out on the couch, which was her temporary bed, she was just dozing off when somebody yanked the blankets off of her. They did not simply slide to the floor, they were clearly *pulled* away. She retrieved the blankets and a short time later it happened again. In fact, the strange game of pulling off the blankets continued throughout the night.

In the days that followed, one of the workmen came up to Mrs. Wilson and told her that in one of the third floor bedrooms he experienced an icy cold spot. He believed that what he had felt was the presence of a ghost. Soon after, a different construction worker who had just arrived and had heard nothing of the strange events also reported to Mrs. Wilson that there were unnatural cold spots in that same third floor bedroom, and he firmly believed the room was haunted.

Another day as she stood in the foyer she heard the loud, pounding footsteps of a man running down the long flights of stairs leading from the third floor. It was an installer from the telephone company who had been working in that cold bedroom. He never broke stride as he shouted to Mrs. Wilson, "That room is haunted, you know!" He continued out the open front door and never returned.

On many occasions, objects that had been left in one room would be found the next day in another part of the house, even when no one else was at home. There was nothing evil or sinister about these events, but it was clear that something was trying to make its presence known. While the Wilson's did not feel threatened or frightened by anything that had happened, their sentiments were not always shared by guests.

One day Mrs. Wilson was showing a visitor the progress of renovations on the third floor. No one else was in the house and the two were standing at the top of the stairs, right next to the mysterious bedroom. Suddenly, there was a loud knocking sound. It came from the wall of the entrance to the room, just a few feet away. There was no one else to be seen, no visible hand that could be knocking on that wall. Completely terrified, the man literally ran down the staircase and out of the house. (Perhaps they should have installed a swinging front door?)

Many members of the Wilson family have spent peaceful nights in the house, with no hint of anything paranormal going on. Then there was the night that Mrs. Wilson's daughter and son-in-law slept in one of the second floor bedrooms. They slept through the night without the slightest sound to disturb them. When the daughter awoke, however, she found that the almost five-foot high solid walnut dresser had been pushed across the floor and was up against the closed bedroom door. Waking up her husband, she asked why in heaven he had barricaded the door with the dresser, and how did he do it without waking her?

One can only imagine the expression on his face as he alternately looked at the displaced dresser and his wife, searching for any sign that this was a joke. She was serious, and so was he. He swore that he had not moved the dresser. Other times when this daughter has come to visit, she has claimed to hear the doors on the second floor opening and slamming shut again, when no living souls were on that floor. A family friend who house-sits on occasion has also reported strange occurrences when no one else is present, like the television in the library turning itself on and off.

Other reports of bizarre activity have made their way to the ears of the Wilsons. One dramatic incident in particular occurred decades ago when the house was being used as a restaurant. At the end of one of the first floor side halls, there was a heavy pay phone mounted on the wall. As a waitress was walking down the hall, the phone suddenly tore loose from the wall and flew across the hall. The waitress was very clear about the incident, the phone did not fall off the wall and hit the floor beneath it. It was as if some unseen hands ripped the telephone from the wall and threw across the hall where it smashed against the opposite wall.

***

Having heard stories about this house being haunted, I contacted Mrs. Wilson and asked if I might come by and take a look, and she graciously consented. The day I arrived was one of the hottest days of that steamy July of 1998, and as I stepped out of the car I would have welcomed a few cold spots. Instead, I was welcomed by the Wilson's four wonderful dogs and had to dispense ample pats all around before we could get down to business.

6

The six of us (Mrs. Wilson, the dogs, and myself) proceeded into the house. They had indeed done a marvelous job of restoring the place, and I almost felt as if I should purchase a ticket before my tour. My first question was to ask when the last odd occurrence had taken place, and was somewhat surprised to find that just the night before, Mrs. Wilson had placed her glasses on a table in the library and then had gone to bed. That morning she went to retrieve them, and they were not to be found anywhere in the room. They had not been pushed under a magazine or newspaper, and they had not been knocked onto the floor by an eager wagging tail. What did happen to them is not exactly known, but she finally found them up on a shelf in the dining room. How they left the table, crossed the hall and made their way to the dining room is just one of the daily mysteries of their home.

As we climbed the stairs to the second floor, the dogs all faithfully followed within a few feet of Mrs. Wilson, like a school of fish that stuck to her like glue. The pink guest bedroom to the right of the top of the landing had been the site of another incident a few days earlier. One morning all the pillows from the bed were found piled up by the door. As usual, there was no explanation. The blue bedroom to the left of the stairs was the room where the dresser had moved during the night. I tried to give the substantial piece of furniture a push, and found that it wouldn't budge without some serious exertion, and noise. I wondered whether the force that had used it to block the door had been trying to keep the couple inside the room, or prevent someone, or something, from entering the room.

As we ascended the staircase to the third floor, the dogs all followed again, to a point. At the top of the stairs the Akita/Labrador mix, Shadow, stopped short. Previously, he had followed his mistress' every footstep, but now as she went to the center of the wide hallway between bedrooms, Shadow just stood by the stairs, refusing to pass in front of the bedroom to the right in which the visitors had experienced the cold spots and terrifying knocking sounds. I stepped around Shadow and entered the room. There was an oppressive feeling of sadness and despair, a heavy atmosphere that almost felt like a physical weight. To put it simply, I did not feel comfortable in the room and left to rejoin Shadow.

At the opposite end of the hall, Mrs. Wilson started to show me another room, but before we could take two steps, the other dogs began to bark and became very agitated. Until coming up to the third floor, they had all been quiet and playful, but now their behavior was completely different. As a lifelong dog lover, I know when a dog does not want to be somewhere. I have found time and again that in addition to keener senses of hearing and smell, dogs also have a strong sixth sense. If a picture is worth a thousand words, then the behavior of these four dogs spoke volumes.

Their hair stood up on the backs of their necks, their postures changed to defensive/fear stances, they began whining and staring at things we could not

7

see and they clearly were urging Mrs. Wilson to leave that third floor. Returning to the ground floor, the dogs immediately calmed down and returned to their relaxed, quiet, tail-wagging behavior.

After a quick tour of the basement, the scientist in me wanted to return to that third floor to repeat the experiment. The dogs faithfully went up the first flight, but this time Shadow wouldn't even go up the stairs to the third floor. A couple of the dogs did follow, but again immediately started to whine, bark and become agitated. As I passed the spot where the knocking sound had been, I put my hand against the wall and discovered it was not wood or plaster, but solid concrete, not the easiest substance with which to create a loud knocking sound with your hand. (You could try it yourself, but I warn you that you generate far more pain than noise.)

We then all went outside and the dogs went straight to playing, rolling in the grass and doing all the things happy, well-loved dogs do. I asked Mrs. Wilson how she felt living in a house where there are almost daily occurrences of the unexplainable, and she quite honestly replied that they were very happy there. They have never felt threatened, and do not think that if there is a presence there, it means anyone any harm. As I drove away, I thought that this was truly one of the most beautiful homes in Rockland, and if living there meant putting up with a few permanent houseguests, then it was worth a little mischief from time to time.

***

There are no hard and fast explanations for what happens in houses like this one, but it is not uncommon that such places have been the site of tragic events. What can be confirmed is that just such an event did occur in the house in the early 1930's. As the country was reeling in the turmoil of the stock market crash, the owner of the house became despondent over his financial situation. He took his own life, committing suicide with a gun in the same third floor bedroom that now produces deathly cold spots, loud noises, and an overwhelmingly sense of sadness and grief. People who claim to be sensitive to such things believe that in addition to the ghost of this man, there are also the spirits of a woman and a small child.

This is a case that truly has more questions than answers. If only dogs could talk.

***

I was saddened to learn that in 2000, Mrs. Wilson passed away. She died at home, and some people claim that her presence can now be felt there. The house is currently up for sale.

COFFEE--IRREGULAR

Grand View-on-Hudson is a tranquil little enclave overlooking the river. There are some beautiful older homes here that hearken back to Rockland's simpler days. Of course, simpler isn't always better. For example, few people today would opt to cook on a coal-burning stove, given the convenience of gas or electric. However, there still may be at least one Grand View resident who still clings to the old ways, even though she and her stove are both long gone...

Soon after new owners moved into their Grand View home, they awoke to the enticing smell of fresh coffee. The only problem was that no one in the family had made any coffee, and nothing could be discovered to explain the distinctive aroma. In the days that followed, they began to hear the sounds of someone crinkling paper and breaking sticks as if preparing a fire. This was followed by an odd sound that would have fit the description of coal being poured out of a bucket into a stove. Shortly after, that wonderful aroma of freshly brewed coffee would fill the house again.

Could this have been a prank by a family member or friend, someone who would go to the trouble of building a fire, make coffee and then leave, removing all evidence? It could have been, except for the nagging little fact that the old coal stove had long ago been removed from the kitchen, with a modern stove installed in its place.

Then there were the sounds of a child playing in the kitchen, happily bouncing a ball. Here again was a problem, as no one was in the kitchen when these sounds were heard.

Given the range of haunting experiences from the benign to the terrifying, these Grand View ghosts definitely rank low on the fiendish scale. Unless, of course, you are one of those coffee addicts who would be tortured by awaking to such a heavenly scent, only to find out that the brew is pure phantom java.

STILL SCREAMING

The beautiful river that flows along the eastern boundary of Rockland County, which the Indians called the Shatemuc, underwent a name change thanks to an English explorer working for the Dutch. Henry Hudson first sailed up the then pristine river in 1609, and in recognition for his achievement this historic waterway now bears his name. One might envy Hudson for being commemorated in such a way, but before you get too green, consider his fate.

Henry Hudson and his ship, the *Half Moon*.

In 1610, Hudson made another voyage to the New World, this time entering the great bay in Canada that would also come to bear his name. After enduring a brutal winter along the shores of the bay, Hudson's long-suffering crew had had enough. They mutinied and set their captain, his son and seven other sailors adrift in a small boat and the abandoned men were never seen again. The story of Hudson's tragic demise was a popular tale to tell amongst the Dutch colonists of early Rockland, and like most stories it became embellished over the years.

Thus the legend of the Ghost Ship of the Hudson was born. The majority of the alleged sightings on the river occurred in stormy weather (perhaps after a few drinks to stave off a chill?), in the general location of the present-day Tappan Zee Bridge. In addition to seeing the shadowy figure of an old Dutch ship, witnesses claimed to be able to hear the screams of the tormented crew in between claps of thunder.

Today, people still hear the screaming, only rather than coming from a ghost ship, it's from commuters stuck in the legendary traffic.

SPANIARDS, SILVER AND MURDER

In the early 1700s, Caldwell's Landing (now Jones' Point in Tomkins Cove) was a popular stop for sailors on their journeys up and down the Hudson River. Ships anchored here not to take in the natural beauty of the place, but rather to visit the tavern and enjoy the specialty of the house, schnapps. When one considers the amount of the potent beverage consumed, the local legends of evil gnomes and ghost ships begin to make sense. However, there is one legend that may have some basis in fact.

In the early summer of 1720, a Spanish ship anchored near the tavern. Dark-haired men with scowling faces left the ship carrying picks and shovels. The local men could see that these visitors were not there for drinks and conversation, and fearing for their own safety, simply watched in silence as the strangers headed into the woods. Months passed before these men were seen again. When they finally returned, they were carrying large, heavy sacks. At least one of these men brought his sack into the tavern for a little liquid nourishment before setting sail.

As the schnapps began to loosen the stranger's tongue, he began to talk about what he and his comrades had been doing all summer. He then revealed the contents of his burden to one of the locals. It was filled with what looked like silver ore, and if the metal was indeed genuine, the strangers had made themselves a small fortune. Wasting no more time, the strangers boarded their ship and sailed away with their treasure. No doubt as soon as the ship was out of sight, some of the local men went into the woods in an attempt to discover the Spanish silver mine, but found nothing.

Some time later, while hunting on Black Mountain, a couple of men came across a crude, uninhabited cabin. The cabin had two small rooms and a porch that was built at an angle to the rest of the structure. This porch was constructed so that it faced the top of the mountain, as if to give the occupants a clear view of something important. Believing that this was where the entrance to the Spanish silver mine must be, the hunters scoured the area but could find no opening.

A year or two later, the Spaniards returned with empty sacks and their picks and shovels. Again, after several months, they returned laden with valuable silver ore. This continued for several more years, until finally some of the men in the tavern confronted the strangers and demanded to know what was going on. Obviously, if there was a fortune to be made in their own backyards, they wanted a piece of it. The Spaniards, however, were not

Black Mountain and Silver Mine Lake.

11

in the mood to share and when the argument threatened to turn violent, the local men backed down and let the six strangers go on their way.

Summer once again drew to a close, but this time only two of the men returned. They immediately got on their ship and sailed away. Unable to contain their curiosity, two of the local men hurried to the cabin on Black Mountain, on the pretense that they were concerned for the other strangers. Hoping to finally find the opening to the mine, or perhaps some sacks of silver left behind, they entered the cabin. They were not prepared for the horrible scene that they discovered inside.

Instead of gleaming silver they found bloody red—the bodies of two murdered men lay on the floor. One had had his skull broken, while the other had a Spanish dagger buried deep in his chest. After they overcame the shock, the men realized that two other strangers were still missing. Although darkness was falling, they headed toward the summit of the mountain in search of the missing men. (Of course, if they happened to find the opening to the mine, that would be even better.) However, what they found, or what found them, was even more terrifying than the bloody scene in the cabin.

As the last rays of sunlight fell beneath the horizon, a strange light appeared. The men froze as the light rushed toward them and they could see that it was actually the eerily glowing forms of the missing Spaniards. The men tried to run, but their muscles seemed to turn to stone and they were unable to move. The spirits howled and swirled around them all night and the terrified men were forced to watch this horrifying dance of the dead.

When the first light of dawn touched the top of Black Mountain, the ghosts suddenly vanished and the men were able to move. They did not hesitate to use the opportunity to run as fast as their still-chilled limbs could carry them, and they made a bee-line to the tavern to tell their tale of horror. Their friends laughed at the story of the ghosts, but those who bravely ventured near the summit of Black Mountain came back with the same frightening story of the swirling apparitions.

Many years later the town of Queensboro was built on the north side of Black Mountain. To the new inhabitants, the old legends of the murdered Spaniards were considered to be nothing more than foolish stories to frighten children, but when hunters found that their dogs became afraid and ran from the area that was supposed to be haunted, some of them decided to take a closer look. Whatever it was that they found convinced many to hunt elsewhere.

The Spaniards' cabin long ago decayed to nothingness, and the town of Queensboro is also gone, but the legend lives on. To this day, visitors to Silver Mine park occasionally cannot resist the lure of lost treasure, and hike back to Black Mountain hoping to find the opening to the mine which cost the lives of at least four men. Geologists do admit that silver could exist in these mountains, but so far no one has uncovered any large deposits.

The stories of ghosts and silver may be hard to believe, so perhaps the best way to prove whether the legends are true or not, is for you to put on your hiking boots and take a look for yourself. But if it is a late summer's day and the deepening shadows of the setting sun reveal a pair of glowing lights headed your way, don't say you haven't been warned.

***

In recent years, authorities were alerted to strange noises coming from Black Mountain. Park rangers and police went to investigate and they apprehended a couple of over-eager treasure hunters who believed the legends of Spanish silver and were using dynamite to try to locate the old mine.

(A friendly warning; this is not only dangerous, but quite illegal, and anyone attempting such a stunt will be arrested. Handling dynamite is also a good way to turn yourself into a ghost.)

SPOOK ROCK

It is interesting to note how many ghost stories in Rockland actually involve rocks. One of the oldest of these is on Spook Rock Road in Airmont, and over the generations this story has acquired so many variations that only two elements remain consistent—a rock and a ghost.

Spook is an old Dutch term meaning spirit and the story does involve some of the earliest Dutch settlers in the county. As the story goes, one of the settlers committed some kind of crime against the local Indian population; something even worse than the usual ill treatment native peoples often received. Whatever the deed, the result was that the long-suffering Indians decided to seek revenge. They kidnapped the young daughter of the offending settler and brought her to the rock, which they used for ceremonies. At the time there was a cave beneath the rock and the top of the rock had a large indentation that would have been ideal for a large bonfire.

After conducting the appropriate revenge ceremony (which may or may not have involved dancing and chanting depending upon the version one hears) the innocent girl was brutally sacrificed on the rock. Almost immediately after the terrible deed was done, members of the tribe learned that the settler was not guilty of the crime for which he had been accused. This left the chief with terrible feelings of guilt and remorse, and some versions of the story say that the ghost of the murdered girl haunted him every night of his life, visible only to him.

There is also a version that claims that the girl's spirit was seen by all the members of the tribe, hovering over the rock where her unjust death occurred, either strictly on the anniversary of the sacrifice, or every night until every member of the tribe had died. Her ghost was described as being everything from a simple glowing form drifting above the rock, to a vengeful, angry spirit that drew people like an irresistible magnet, never allowing a peaceful night for the rest of their lives.

In more modern times, some people claimed to have seen a ghostly figure hovering above the rock. These sightings have most often occurred around Halloween, the time around which the legend claims the sacrifice took place. Many local residents have also insisted that the road leading to the rock has an eerie feeling to it. This in part was the result of the illusion that cars could roll uphill, as if being pulled toward the rock. However, since improvements to the road were made and the area became more developed, the reports of this magnetic attraction have diminished.

Is there any truth to the tale of the murdered girl? Is something strange and otherworldly linked for all eternity to this ancient ceremonial rock? Take a look sometime in the dead of night, and discover the truth for yourself.

Modern roads have encroached on Spook Rock,
which is now reinforced with bricks and concrete.

THE BABYSITTER'S NIGHTMARE

Babysitting is one of those jobs that when it goes right it is a piece of cake—the children are well-behaved, they go to bed on time, and you get to watch television and get paid for it. However, babysitting can also be the worst of jobs—unruly children who refuse to go to bed and seem determined to make those hours as miserable as possible.

Then there is Hollywood's version of babysitting—a knife-wielding nightmare that usually ends up with more buckets of fake blood and dismembered manikins than you can count.

But what about the real nightmares? What about the poor babysitter who must sit up half the night in a strange house keeping company with a spirit of the undead?

***

It was the 1970s, "Julie" and "Christine" were in high school, and they were looking forward to their babysitting assignment on Saturday night. They would be going to Julie's aunt and uncle's house to watch their seven-year-old daughter, Janice. Janice was well-behaved, the refrigerator would be well-stocked and this was a chance for them to be on their own for a few hours.

Julie's uncle picked up the two girls and brought them to his home in what is now Chestnut Ridge. It was a beautiful old farmhouse shaded by stately trees, with a huge stone fireplace and a large front porch overlooking a rolling lawn. They entered through the back door and Christine immediately felt at home in the warm and inviting old-fashioned kitchen. It was the type of feeling you would get in your grandmother's home, a sensation so strong that it almost felt like a presence, a very soothing presence.

Julie's aunt and uncle gave their final instructions regarding Janice's bedtime, the phone number of where they could be reached, and most importantly, the location of all the snack foods. After the adults left for their party, Julie and Christine successfully kept Janice amused until she went to bed, and then they set to making a large bowl of popcorn and a pitcher of iced tea. They took their snack and drinks into the parlor and Christine immediately felt a chill as she entered the room, but since it was an old house, cold drafts were to be expected. Besides, it would be a good excuse to start a fire in the fireplace, thereby providing the perfect opportunity to toast marshmallows.

The parlor was typical of 19th century farmhouses and was decorated accordingly. The fireplace was on the west wall of the room, the south wall had the doorway that led down a narrow hall to the kitchen, the north wall had a window looking out toward the road and the east wall had a large bay window overlooking the porch.

The fire was soon burning brightly, but as the two friends sat on the couch under the bay window talking all about their friends and school, Christine continued to feel cold and uncomfortable. Several times she lost track of the conversation because she felt as if someone was on the porch watching them, and she would quickly turn her head, only to see nothing. She was reluctant to tell Julie about the eerie feeling, because she didn't want her friend to think she had silly, childish fears of the dark, or that she was afraid of being away from home. Christine was actually a very independent girl who enjoyed being outside at night, and she didn't flinch at creaking tree limbs or animals rustling through the underbrush. But this was different, very different.

After about an hour, the phone rang in the kitchen and Julie went to answer it. It was her mother checking to see if everything was all right. As Christine sat by herself in the parlor, she watched the red and orange flames dancing around the crackling logs and tried to convince herself that she had simply seen too many horror movies and she was letting her imagination get the best of her. But as she finally began to relax and settle into the cozy couch, a cold rush of air swept over her from behind, making the hairs stand up on the back of her neck and arms.

Was that the sound of heavy footsteps coming up the porch stairs? Was that someone running up to the window, straight toward her? With a gasp and half-choked scream, Christine leaped up from the couch and spun around, fully expecting to see a madman with murderous intent, with only thin panes of glass separating them.

There was no one in sight. The porch was fully lit, so no one could be concealed in a shadow, and no one would have had time to get away without being seen in the split second it took Christine to turn and look out.

Not wanting to spend another second in that parlor, Christine hurried back into the kitchen, where the soothing feeling helped calm her, but not completely. Julie was still on the phone with her mother, and didn't notice how pale her friend was, or how she was breathing heavily and trembling. But after she hung up the phone, she saw Christine's expression and asked what was the matter. Christine hesitated, but only for a moment.

"You might think I'm crazy, but I am not going back into that room!" she stated unequivocally.

"Why not, what happened?" Julie responded with intense interest, and no hint of ridicule.

"I swear someone was watching me. And I heard…and I…I felt a man rushing toward me across the porch. I *know* he wanted to hurt me," Christine replied, unsuccessfully suppressing a shudder. "I know this sounds stupid, but I *won't* go back in there."

Christine waited for what she thought would at least be some good-natured kidding, but Julie's face was serious. Dead serious.

"I know what you mean. That room gives me the creeps, too. That's why I asked you to come with me tonight," Julie confessed. "I didn't want to be alone in this house."

"Oh, that's just great!" Christine said, relieved and annoyed at the same time. "Now you tell me."

Julie went on to explain that her aunt and uncle never mentioned anything strange going on in the house, but she did notice that they hadn't been the happy couple they were before moving in. She didn't know the history of the old house, but she wasn't sure she wanted to know, either. Then Julie hurried into the parlor to retrieve the glasses and popcorn bowl, and the two girls spent the rest of the night in the comforting kitchen, always keeping one eye on the hallway that led to the parlor. When Julie's aunt and uncle finally came home, they said nothing about the unseen presence, because they didn't want their parents to think they were too young to go out on their own again.

Weeks passed and the incident was soon forgotten in the swirl of school, homework and boys. Then one Saturday Julie's mother asked her to go to her aunt's house. The family had gone out of town to a party and her aunt had baked two cakes, one for the party and one for Julie's family. Julie immediately called Christine.

"But you have to go with me! The cake is on the kitchen table, and all we have to do is take two steps in through the back door, grab the cake and get out of there." Julie pleaded with her friend until she relented.

The sun had just dipped below the horizon when Julie and Christine entered the dark driveway and stopped by the back door. Against her better judgment, Christine followed Julie into the kitchen. That soothing grandmotherly presence greeted them again, and both girls suddenly felt very foolish about their fears. But as Julie picked up the cake and they turned to leave, they heard something they will never forget—an unearthly, tormented cry coming from the parlor which contained no one. No one alive, that is.

"It was a man's scream…a terrible moaning, groaning, tortured scream," Christine explained, still visibly shaken by the event that had occurred decades earlier. "It was just like something you would hear in a horror movie, only you did more than hear it, you *felt* it; an icy, deathly feeling. It was the most terrifying thing I have ever experienced.

"At first Julie and I didn't move, we just looked at each other, I guess to make sure we were both hearing the same thing. Then we ran. I never again set foot in that house, and to this day I get goose bumps just driving by it."

Soon after the frightening incident, Julie's aunt and uncle got a divorce and sold the house. She was upset over the divorce, but glad she would never have to go back to that place again. Neither Julie nor Christine know if the new owners have ever felt the comforting presence in the kitchen, or experienced the terrifying, moaning spirit of the porch and parlor, but then, neither of them cared to go back to the house to find out.

CAT'S EYES

Science has attested to the fact that some animals have vastly superior hearing and senses of smell, but do they also possess an extrasensory perception that most humans lack? Many accounts of haunted homes involve pets who stare intently at what appears to be thin air, or growl and become agitated and run away from an unseen presence. Some people might laugh at this idea, but in one such case that occurred in a cemetery in Blauvelt, the two young women involved didn't find it very funny.

"Sharon" was taking a course in photography and needed to take some black and white photos. Finding that cemeteries provided the contrast and shadows for which she was looking, Sharon loaded her camera and tried to decide the best locations in the county. Calling her friend "Ann," she suggested that they take advantage of the warm spring weather and make a day of it. Ann had recently gotten a kitten, Max, and she didn't want to leave him alone, so the three set out on an adventure they thought would simply be a pleasant time taking pictures and soaking up sunshine. What they got was more than they could ever have imagined.

Their first stop was an old cemetery on Western Highway in Blauvelt. While Ann watched Max chase butterflies and bat leaves through the rows of graves, Sharon looked for the right angles for her photos. For some unknown reason, Sharon was drawn to one tombstone in particular, and she found it curious that the unusual last name on the stone was the same as her own. Mentioning this to Ann, her friend came to look, calling for Max to follow. The frolicking kitten came bounding over, then suddenly stopped short next to the grave. The previously playful animal arched his back, his hair stood on end and he began hissing and making threatening noises.

Ann remarked that she had never seen Max act that way before. The two women looked all around, but could see no reason for the kitten's unusual reaction. Ann picked up Max and carried him to another section of the cemetery. As soon as he was placed on the ground, he was back to his old self, leaping and running as if nothing had happened. The two women were beginning to feel very uncomfortable, but tried to laugh it off as just a silly coincidence. Just to prove to themselves that there was nothing supernatural about that one grave, Ann brought Max back to the area where he had reacted in such a bizarre fashion.

Max started to chase a fly, but once again stopped short when he came to the grave. Back arched, hair raised, he hissed menacingly, his eyes fixed upon something only he could see. The kitten backed slowly away, never taking his eyes off whatever it was that was provoking such fear. This second episode was more than the nerves of the two women could stand, and picking up Max, they hurried back to the car.

As they drove away, Sharon decided that she would chose another subject for her photography assignment—the living, breathing, very visible kitten who's eyes might just have glimpsed something beyond the grave.

LAVENDER

During the late 1940s, two juniors from Hamilton College were driving through western Rockland to a dance in Tuxedo Park. Although autumn was fast approaching, it had been one of those beautiful, warm days that can make you forget that a cold wind will soon be blowing dead, dry leaves across a barren landscape.

It was just after sunset and the road was leading the young men north along the path of the Ramapo River. Against the backdrop of the darkening sky, their headlights suddenly caught the figure of a young girl wearing a long, sparkling, lavender dress. The color of the sequined evening gown matched her vibrant eyes and complemented her golden hair.

Immediately hitting the brakes, the two students asked the girl if she needed a ride, or if they could be of any assistance. With a charming smile, she replied that she was going to a square dance at Sterling Furnace. After some friendly discussions about which would be the better dance to attend, the young men convinced the lovely stranger to accompany them to Tuxedo Park. When the trio arrived, the girl introduced herself as Lavender, explaining that it wasn't her real name, merely a nickname because she always wore that color.

Lavender proved to be a delightful guest, and although she was not very talkative, she did display great skill at dancing—particularly the older dances which proved a challenge to others her age. There was one other odd thing— Lavender's skin felt a bit cold to the touch, but then her thin dress couldn't have provided much warmth.

When the dance finally drew to a close, the two young men were more than happy to offer Lavender a ride home. Once outside, it was clear that autumn had betrayed itself in the evening chill, and having no other garments than the sequined dress, the girl shivered pitifully. Proving that chivalry (at least) was not dead, one of the young men quickly offered his tweed overcoat to Lavender.

The way to the girl's home proved to be a challenge along winding, unpaved country roads, but the young men didn't mind as long as they were in this captivating girl's presence. However, some of her Cinderella charm must have been tarnished when she finally told them to stop the car. There before them, dimly illuminated by the car's headlights, was a broken-down shack that looked abandoned, or if it wasn't, should have been long ago. The only sign that the shack wasn't inhabited strictly by vermin was in the form of a dirty and torn lace curtain.

Lavender, apparently undaunted by her overly humble surroundings, cheerfully promised she would meet the boys again and said her farewells. Making no moves toward actually entering the shack, she just stood near the front door and watched the boys drive off.

A bit overwhelmed by the entire night, the young man who had gallantly offered his coat didn't realize she had not returned it until they were most of the way back to the main road. It was too late to try to find the shack again, especially in the dark without directions, so they decided to return the following afternoon.

Even in bright sunshine it was not easy finding Lavender's home. Finally, they stopped in front of the dilapidated hovel where they had left the girl in the sequined dress the night before. When they knocked on the door, an ancient-looking woman answered, and asked what they wanted. Still maintaining their air of chivalry, they said nothing of the previous evening, and simply declared that they were old friends coming to call.

The old woman eyed them suspiciously, but then responded, "You must be real old friends not to know that Lavender ain't lived here for ten years now."

The young men patiently tried to explain to the old woman that she must be mistaken, that in truth they had just seen Lavender the night before.

"You couldn't have seen Lavender," the woman stated adamantly. The young men persisted until she added, "I'm telling you boys you ain't seen Lavender. She ain't lived here in years because she's been dead. Dead and buried all these ten years."

Stunned, the young men didn't know what to say. They could not believe the old woman, she couldn't possibly be telling the truth. They had seen Lavender. They had talked with her, danced with her in their arms...

"You know Lavender weren't even her real name. Her real name was Lily, but people got to callin' her Lavender cause that lavender, sparkly dress was the only thing she ever wore. She died in that dress. And she is buried in that dress just down the road a piece."

The two dazed college boys half-staggered back to their car, not knowing what to believe, not knowing what to do, until they came upon the lonely, neglected graveyard down the dirt road. The driver stopped the car, and they looked at one another, silently testing their level of courage. Then the driver said what they were both thinking.

"We have to take a look. We have to know."

Amidst a tangle of vines and thick weeds, the two young men did find a simple gravestone, its only mark, the name "Lily" carved into the cold rock. There in the shadow of the tiny monument to a life cut short, they saw something else—the tweed overcoat, carefully folded and placed for the boys Lavender had promised to see again.

***

According to a former postmaster in the area, there was a young girl named Lily who earned quite a reputation at a tender age. She was often seen in the company of boys—boys who would skip Sunday school to pick wild berries with her in the hills of western Rockland. Whether such behavior warranted a reputation remains to be seen, and if there was more to the story no one spelled it out.

Regardless of the actual situation, there was a charming girl named Lily and she did come from a very poor family. She had but one tattered dress, and when the local church was handing out donated clothing, Lily shyly watched from the back of the room. She overcame her shyness, however, when from out of a barrel was pulled a long, sequined, lavender evening gown. To a girl who lived in a shack and wore rags, it must have appeared to be the most beautiful thing she had ever seen. To the preacher and members of the congregation, the flashy, low-cut dress must have been nothing short of shocking.

Previously, every scrap of clothing had been hotly contested. Now, no one spoke. Lily didn't speak either, but she did walk quickly to the front of the church and take the dress from the preacher's hand. From that day forward, it was the only thing she ever wore, regardless of the weather, season or time of day. Also from that day, she was known as Lavender.

Early one December, Lavender's cousins in New Jersey sent her money to take the bus and come and visit them. One can only imagine the reactions when Lavender stepped onto the bus in her evening gown, and whatever scornful, unkind remarks the people in town might have said about her going on a trip dressed like that, it would be their last opportunity to do so. That day would be the last time anyone in town saw her alive.

Upon returning home two weeks later, the bus driver dropped her off on the main road late at night. Lavender started to walk toward home, but the weather was unusually cold, with the temperature plummeting to -18 degrees. Such temperatures can be dangerous to people dressed in overcoats, hats and gloves. To a young girl clad only in a flimsy evening gown, they are deadly.

Early the next morning, Lavender's frozen, lifeless body was found on the side of the road. It was the same spot where ten years later, two young college men stopped to pick up a girl in a sequined, lavender evening gown...

SPIRIT OF HOOK MOUNTAIN

In the 18th century, there was a Native American named Comboan living in the woods of Nyack, where Brookside and Clinton Avenues are today. He was a skilled tracker and hunter and knew every inch of land for miles around. The transplanted European residents of Nyack liked and trusted Comboan, and often asked for his help, which he always graciously gave.

One night they asked for Comboan's help in a matter of life and death. Two small children had wandered away from the village and had become lost in the black depths of the forest. Even though they had been gone for three days and there had been heavy rains that would have washed away their footprints, Comboan immediately put his years of tracking experience to work. Crawling, stretching, bending, searching for any signs of the missing children, he finally picked up their trail. Comboan found the children. They were cold, exhausted and half-starved, but they were alive.

There was a great celebration, with everyone thanking the old tracker for saving the lives of the missing children. Thinking they were offering a wonderful gift, the parents of the children offered to have Comboan baptized into the Christian religion. Comboan's people had always worshipped the Great Spirit that they believed resided in the area below Hook Mountain, and he politely declined. He was a man of the woods and his faith was in the spirits who dwelt there.

While Comboan kept his faith, the residents of Nyack cruelly broke theirs. With the onset of the French and Indian War in the 1750s, people began to become suspicious of any Native American. Their imaginations ran wild, and they came up with the implausible story that Comboan was planning to slaughter them all in their sleep. The people of Nyack went so far as to put Comboan on trial for his alleged plot. He, of course, declared his innocence. The people were unconvinced. He talked of the many times he was asked to help the settlers, and of how he had saved the lives of two of their children. The people were unmoved.

Comboan was sentenced to a fate worse than death—banishment from his beloved Nyack, forced to leave the land of his ancestors and the Great Spirit. Soon after the old man was driven from his home and out of the county, it was reported that he had died, perhaps of a broken heart. Many years later, however, people smelled burning wood and saw wisps of a campfire smoke coming from the area where Comboan used to hunt. No fires could be found, but they did find hunting traps that no one but Comboan could have devised. They also began to see moccasin prints where no one had walked. Perhaps it was their collective guilt that made them experience these things, or perhaps Comboan's spirit had returned to the land he loved.

The rugged cliffs of Hook Mountain overlook
the woods that Comboan once called home.

For years, people were too afraid to walk in the fields and down the paths by Hook Mountain where Comboan had lived, giving the area the name Spook Hollow. As time passed, however, the legend of the old man faded from memory and progress brought developments to the once wild forests of Nyack. Yet even in this century, there have been strange things going on at the base of that mountain. Several people, unaware of the stories of the past, spoke of seeing an old Indian offering prayers skyward. Others told of soft footsteps following them, almost as if the person was wearing moccasins, but no one could be seen.

Today, with all the picnickers, hikers and cyclists jamming the park at Hook Mountain, and jet skiers buzzing up and down the river, it's hard to imagine a time when the area was peaceful and unspoiled. If you do happen to find a quiet evening to take a walk beneath the rugged mountains, pause for a moment and try to picture the land as Comboan knew it. In those last amber rays of sunlight, you might also want to check the ground for moccasin prints, sniff the air for smoke, and as you walk back to your car, remember that you might not be alone.

THE FIRST LEGAL HAUNTING

In July of 1991, the New York State Supreme Court Appellate Division voted on an issue that made headlines around the world. This was not a case of murder, kidnapping, blackmail or grand larceny. This case involved a real estate deal on La Veta Place in Nyack. The vote was 3-2 in favor of the plaintiffs, and the decision read as follows: "As a matter of law, the house is haunted."

Ghost hunters around the world were ecstatic—here was finally some official recognition of what they had believed all along. Here, in Nyack, was the world's first legal haunting. What led to this remarkable ruling by the court? What was at stake, and what were the repercussions of this decision? And, most importantly, who were these history-making ghosts?

The story begins in the 1960s, when Helen Ackley moved into her large Victorian home, built in 1900, on La Veta Place. One of the first signs that the place was haunted was the sound of footsteps on the staircase, when no one could be seen. Then there were the hanging lights in the dining room that on occasion would swing vigorously back and forth, when not so much as a light breeze was present.

Such occurrences would make most people reconsider their place of residence, but Mrs. Ackley never felt threatened. Even the children seemed to adhere to the policy of peaceful coexistence, which is remarkable considering that whenever Mrs. Ackley's son seemed poised to oversleep on a school morning, his bed would be violently shaken at exactly 7:15am. This was the time he was supposed to get up, and the helping hands that took it upon themselves to keep the boy from being late to school, were as invisible as thin air.

There were some guests, however, who were not so comfortable with the La Veta Place spirits, especially when they encountered unnaturally cold spots, either by passing through a deathly cold area in a hall or room, or having a chilling mass of air pass through them as they stood or were seated. And when a ghostly figure of an 18th century man, replete with powdered wig, appeared to one guest it was more than her nerves could handle. A wispy figure of a woman in a hooded cloak was also seen. Things that go bump are one thing, see-through apparitions are an entirely different matter.

There was also some very solid evidence of a haunting, if we are to believe Mrs. Ackley's rather bizarre accounts. She claimed that the spirits left gifts for her children on two separate occasions. These gifts were very real and very precious—precious as in gold, that is. Mrs. Ackley was convinced that the appearance of two rings, which coincided with special events in her children's lives, were actually materialized by the spirits as a show of their affection.

Even though Helen Ackley and her family were not disturbed by these visitations, she was naturally curious as to the identities of these friendly ghosts. A psychic was called in and she identified these spirits as Sir George and Lady Margaret, an English couple who had died in the 1750s, and had been "commuting between the spirit world and Nyack" ever since. While such a commute is no doubt much easier than using the Tappan Zee Bridge, it's not clear why they picked this particular house in America. Or, had they actually picked Mrs. Ackley?

In the early 1990s, regardless of her ghostly extended family, Mrs. Ackley decided to sell the lovely Victorian. A young couple thought it would be the perfect home, and agreed to pay a $32,500 down payment as part of the deal. It wasn't until after the money had changed hands, though, that the couple was told that their intended home was haunted. The wife was not amused, and quickly decided she could not live under such

conditions. Mrs. Ackley tried to explain that they were friendly ghosts, but this didn't help matters. The couple wanted their $32,500 back. Mrs. Ackley said no. It was now time for the truly frightening part of the story. It was now time for lawyers and lawsuits.

The case eventually made its way to the New York Supreme Court Appellate Division in July of 1991. The judges who received the case were no doubt not very pleased with the prospect of having to make a legal ruling on the existence of ghosts. Such a decision could literally haunt them for the remainder of their careers. Despite the awkward situation, they carefully considered both viewpoints—the couple argued that it had not been disclosed to them that they would not be moving into a vacant house, while Mrs. Ackley explained that although she had no doubt the home was haunted, they were nice ghosts who wouldn't harm anyone.

It was a difficult decision, but the court ruled that if Mrs. Ackley truly believed that disembodied spirits roamed the corridors, shook beds and light fixtures and materialized gifts, she should have disclosed this information to any potential buyer who may not share her enthusiasm for sharing their home with the dead. Their 3-2 decision, "As a matter of law, the house is haunted," resulted in Mrs. Ackley being obligated to return the $32,500 down payment.

One can only imagine the tumult this decision caused in both the real estate business, and among the ghost-faithful. Articles appeared around the world, and for a brief fifteen minutes of fame, Nyack was put on the world map. Those who believe in ghosts could now wave the decision high, and declare that this was the proof the skeptics had always demanded. Homeowners were less enthusiastic. They were afraid that any nervous buyer could back out of a deal on the claim that they felt the house was haunted.

Once again, legal action needed to be taken. According to a local realtor, reforms to the rules were enacted and owners and real estate agents now do not have to disclose whether a property is haunted. Also, believing that the house you have committed to buying is haunted, does not give legal grounds for backing out of a deal and recovering your down payment. However, some realtors have been told that they must reveal any evidence of a ghost. Apparently, the issue has yet to be fully clarified, and varies from state to state.

The end result of this incredible case? Buyer beware, as always.

So if you are in the market for a new home, you might want to add a name to your list of pre-contract engineers and house inspectors. You may want to have your friendly neighborhood psychic inspect the spiritual health of your home. It may save you many sleepless nights as you lay awake listening to things going bump…

Epilogue: The house was returned to the market, and many potential buyers (including The Amazing Kreskin) were driven by curiosity to see the place first-hand. It was eventually sold, Helen Ackley moved away, and apparently took her ghosts with her. To date, the most frightening things with which the new owners have had to contend are the school and property taxes.

MARIA'S ROCK

In the days when Rockland consisted of tiny villages, sprawling farms and vast stretches of wilderness, a little girl named Maria picked up a basket and went to gather wild berries. It was a warm, inviting summer's day, and the reds and purples of the plump, ripe berries dotted the forest as far as she could see. So absorbed was Maria in finding the biggest and sweetest fruit, she didn't realize that she had wandered far from her home.

Maria called for her mother, but the only response was the sounds of the forest. She walked faster, then began to run, but in the tangle of underbrush and heavily wooded terrain, there was no way to tell which direction was home, and which direction took her deeper into danger. Exhausted, Maria climbed atop a large rock and cried herself to sleep.

By nightfall, Maria's mother frantically searched everywhere, calling her daughter's name over and over again. The only response was the lonely sounds of the forest.

It wasn't until autumn that they found Maria. She still lay atop the large rock, tatters of her dress still clinging to her bleached bones. For many years after, people passing by the rock could hear the sound of a young girl crying.

Local children put flowers on Maria's Rock, trying to ease the suffering of the lost girl's spirit, but still the weeping continued.

As time passed, the wilderness disappeared. The land upon which rests Maria's Rock became the site for the sprawling Lederle Laboratories complex in Pearl River. Next time you are driving down Middletown Road on an inviting summer's evening, listen carefully as you pass the rock that is just a few steps from the road. If you don't hear the sound of a young girl crying, perhaps it is because Maria has finally made it home.

Generations of people claim to have heard a young girl crying on Maria's Rock.

THE ETERNAL MUSIC OF BACH

We know that music soothes the savage beast, but can it also soothe the lost soul? Apparently so, according to a resident of an early 1800s Dutch home in Grand View.

"Mr. and Mrs. Clements" settled into their new home with their two young children. Mr. Clements worked late hours at his business, leaving Mrs. Clements alone most nights. Every evening after Mrs. Clements put the children to bed, she would spend these peaceful hours practicing the piano. One night, as she played Bach's two-part inventions, she heard footsteps in an upstairs bedroom. The Clements used the room as a guest bedroom, but it originally had been the master bedroom. In any event, no one should have been in there, and she suspected one of the children was wandering when he should be sleeping.

The footsteps then moved to the top of the stairs, and she heard the gentle sound of someone very light on his/her feet descending. Pulling her hands from the keyboard, she turned to confront one of her children, but no one was there. Quietly ascending the stairs, she checked to see if both children were asleep. Waiting several minutes to be sure they were not just pretending to sleep, she went back to her piano wondering if she had just imagined the entire thing. Until it happened again. And again.

On at least eight separate occasions, every time Mrs. Clements began playing the Bach piece, she heard the soft footsteps in the guest bedroom, heard them move to the staircase, and then descend to the bottom step. They always stopped there, as if whatever it was, was forbidden to cross some unseen threshold into the first floor. There were also times when Mrs. Clements was alone in the house, yet heard the soft soprano voice of a young woman. She could neither identify the music, nor its source, but after learning some of the history of the house came to believe that the spirit with the excellent taste in music was that of a French woman who had occupied the home in the late 19th century.

What was the Clements' reaction to these phenomena? Mrs. Clements felt very comfortable with her musically inclined ghost, and actually experienced a warm feeling from its presence. Mr. Clements was another story. He became angry at the slightest mention that they might have a ghost, and refused to discuss it.

There was one incident, however, with which Mrs. Clements was not comfortable. In fact, she was downright terrified. One night as she played, she heard the customary footsteps, but this time there was something different—frighteningly different. The footsteps did not stop when they reached the bottom of the staircase. The footsteps continued in her direction, and it was clear that whatever it was, was moving straight toward her. Hands shaking, she continued to play, hoping it would just go away as it had always done. But it didn't. The footsteps came up right behind her, and then a small hand rested on her shoulder.

As she was about to scream, the innocent voice of her daughter said, "Mommy, can I have a drink of water?"

INDIAN ROCK

One day in January of 1998, I was doing some work while I had the radio on in the background. I had recently decided to write my first ghost book and was on the lookout for new stories. However, I had not expected to find one on the radio.

The station was playing music of the 1930s and 40s, with all too frequent breaks for commercials. I was preoccupied with what I was doing, but vaguely heard some advertisement for a bank on Route 59 in Suffern. My preoccupation suddenly turned to rapt attention, however, when the DJ said, "And don't worry, this bank isn't haunted like the McDonald's across the street. But I'm sure you have heard all about that."

My thoughts began to race; why hadn't I heard anything about this, and was it a nasty McPoltergeist or just some cold spots around the milkshake machine?

The McDonald's on Route 59 in Suffern.
Indian Rock is on the right in the background.

When questioned, the manager and staff claimed that nothing unusual had happened at the fast food restaurant since it had opened the previous August, except that for some unknown reason, business wasn't as good as it had been when it was across the street. I decided to visit the place myself and bring along a psychic who specialized in ghostly occurrences. The only problem was, I didn't know any. I made a few calls and lo and behold, I came across Martha Piesco Hoff. She and her husband, Lawrence, teach spiritual healing in Piermont, and they also have experience in dealing with haunted houses. I explained to Martha that I was writing a book, had heard about a new McDonald's that might be haunted, and asked if she would like to take a field trip.

Enthusiastically agreeing, we arranged to meet in the parking lot one cold, clear winter's morning. I arrived early to take some pictures, and noticed that the new fast food restaurant was on the corner of a large vacant lot, kept company by only a very large boulder. There was a tall sign with an image of the rock, and the name Indian Rock. There were spaces for many store names, but only McDonald's kept the sign from being completely blank.

Martha arrived promptly at the appointed time, and after a brief introduction, we decided to go right inside to warm up. Over some fresh, hot coffee, she asked what I knew about the alleged haunting, and as I began to tell her that I really had no information other then what I had heard on the radio, one of the food machines began to beep. I raised my voice to continue, when a few more machines started beeping and buzzing, creating quite a din. I began to speak even louder, when I paused for a moment and then said to Martha, "Do you realize that anything that can possibly make noise in this place started doing so as soon as you mentioned a haunting?"

Before she could reply, the sounds all abruptly stopped, whether by the hands of an efficient staff, or something else which had so efficiently made its presence known. Taking advantage of the silence, Martha put her sixth sense to work. She said she felt an energy coming from the rock, flowing across the parking lot and passing through the McDonald's right through the entrance. In addition, there were several spirits of Native Americans, most prominently that of a 19-year-old boy who she felt was angry with the developer and was intent on causing mischief.

Indian Rock is now surrounded by a shopping center.

Martha paused a few moments as if having a conversation only she could hear, and then continued, saying that he and the other spirits were angry with the developer because he did not respect their culture. She felt that the development would not prosper until the attitude toward their heritage was changed to one of respect.

We then took a walk near the enormous boulder at the center of the lot. Martha felt that this rock was also at the center of the problem, that it had been an area sacred to the Native Americans for many generations. I mentioned that we were not far from another famous rock, Spook Rock, and she felt that the energy flowed from that direction, through this area, and then off to a roughly southwesterly direction. She talked about some of the other spirits around the rock, and also added that they had a concern for the water quality in the area, but whether that was a concern from the past, or warning for the future was not clear.

I thanked Martha for a most interesting morning, and arrived back home determined to get more information on Indian Rock and the development. Perhaps I was working backwards, perhaps I should have called the local historian first. But if I had known the whole story and had briefed Martha before we had gone on our field trip, it would not have been nearly as remarkable a story that unfolded.

Checking my county historian roster, I found that the man to contact was Craig Long. It so happened that on the day I called he was at home. He was at home due to a bad cold, but generously offered to answer my questions. I briefly told him about the ghost book, and asked what he knew about Indian Rock. Although Craig had not heard about any haunting, he did tell me a very interesting story that fit with what Martha had sensed.

Apparently when the developer had requested approval to build on the site, it was with the understanding that the rock remain intact. While there was no definitive archaeological evidence that the rock was the site of an Indian settlement, or that the rock was sacred, it was fairly certain that this huge hunk of stone was a landmark on an old Indian trail. The trail came from upstate, passed Spook Rock, to Indian Rock and on to the tribal meeting place in Mahwah (which just happens to be located to the southwest of Indian Rock, the direction in which Martha sensed the direction of the flow of energy). It was also a local landmark for generations of recent Rocklanders who grew up in the area.

However, despite his previous agreement, once the developer began clearing the land, he quickly came to the opinion that it was only a useless piece of stone that was getting in the way. He decided that rather then work around it, he was going to have Indian Rock pulverized and carted away. (Sounds like a lack of respect to me.) Upon hearing this, Craig Long spearheaded a campaign to save the rock. It would not be an easy task, as the planning board did not seem sympathetic to the cause of preserving history over that of "progress."

The night of the board's vote arrived, and so did Craig, along with over 100 people prepared to speak in favor of saving Indian Rock. No doubt quickly realizing that unhappy voters were not an asset on Election Day, the board agreed that the developer must stick to his earlier promise and keep Indian Rock intact. Construction did then proceed, but for whatever reason, all of the stores slated to be built pulled out of the deal, except for the McDonald's.

At the time of this writing (August 1998), there was still no other structure being built on the Indian Rock lot, although a few construction vehicles seemed to be pushing around some piles of dirt. Have the angry spirits of Native Americans caused these incessant delays, or can the entire chain of events be explained simply as the uncertain world of business?

Once again, it's up to you to decide whether or not the area is haunted. Visit the McDonald's, have some coffee, maybe some fries, and see what you can sense. Can you feel lost spirits passing through the restaurant on the way to their ancient meeting place? Do warriors still guard the area once sacred to them in life? Or, is the most frightening thing at this McDonald's just the number of fat grams per serving?

***

Since this story was first published, several people have said that they have felt or experienced something strange at this McDonald's. The following are the e-mails sent by Mark P. regarding his experience.

Subject: An interesting visit to McDonald's
Date: Wednesday, July 04, 2001 4:46 PM

Linda-
    Just wanted to relate the following little story...
    I work in Suffern and occasionally visit the local McDonald's for lunch (as my ever increasing waistline will attest). On a recent visit I decided to visit the drive-thru. As I entered the lane I noticed a high-pitched whine coming from the speakers of my radio. The sound increased in pitch and volume until it became very annoying. I turned my radio off—with no effect! The sound still came out of the speakers. I tried to think of a cause for the whine—maybe a problem with my van? But why start at just that time? I then thought that the drive-thru microphone was "bleeding" through my radio. Then I remembered that this McD's doesn't have that kind of set-up...customers speak directly to real live people. I looked around the area for new electrical equipment or possibly someone working on power lines—nothing. (I did, however, notice a new sound like that of several car horns honking—hungry people can be very impatient!)
    When I left the restaurant the sound gradually faded and has not returned since. I didn't think much more of it until I recently re-read Ghosts of Rockland County.
    Definitely gave me something to think about.
    Mark P.

I then asked him to give me more information and here is the follow-up e-mail responding to my questions.

The whole thing struck me as pretty unusual, too—though at the time I didn't connect anything supernatural to it. Another thing about all of it that I didn't realize until I e-mailed you...this particular restaurant is the only McD's that I know of that does NOT have any exterior electronics. No microphone, no order confirmation screen, just a menu board. To order, one HAS to speak to the drive-thru attendant. Maybe there are more problems with the area than anyone would like to advertise...

I am 35 and work as an operations manager for a security company. The incident occurred in early May around 1:00 pm. I've thought about it at length but nothing comes to mind that would "trigger" any such occurrence. However, I do have an interest in Native-American history and display a rather large (and authentic) dream catcher from my rear-view window. Maybe someone thought they had found a kindred spirit (pun intended).

Since my boyfriend, Bob, works nearby, he stopped into this McDonald's to ask why they do not have any electronic ordering systems outside. None of the employees knew why.

In March of 2002, I spoke with a resident of the housing development adjacent to the Indian Rock shopping center. Although he had not heard of any of the rumors of ghosts, he said his wife had been having strange experiences from the day they moved in. Every time she goes down to the basement to do laundry, she has the strong and unnerving feeling that someone is watching her.

Perhaps someone is.

If anyone else encounters anything odd at this location, please drop me a line.

THE HAUNTED COUCH

Developers in New City appear determined to outdo one another in building the largest homes in the most sprawling developments. In the midst of all this new construction, a few 18th century stone colonials cling tenaciously to their little plots of land that once stretched out into acres of rich farmland. These stately homes are a refreshing reminder of taste, charm and a quieter time in Rockland's history. They may also be a reminder that the phrase, "Dead and gone," may not be entirely accurate.

One of these old colonials was purchased by the "Wright" family in the 1980s. Soon after moving in, Mrs. Wright was in a hurry to make an appointment and went into the bathroom to quickly comb her hair. Upon entering the bathroom, she encountered the strong scent of a flowery perfume.

"I was in such a rush," she explained, "that I didn't realize at first that I wasn't using any perfume and no one else was home. As I was going back down the hall, it hit me how strange this was and I turned around to find the source of the overpowering scent. When I went back in the bathroom, the perfume scent was gone, and it had just been so strong only a few seconds earlier!"

The Wrights and their children continued to have odd encounters, but understandable in a household with two adults and several children. They would often see a figure in the corner of their eye, only to turn and find no one there. At first, they all just assumed one of the family members was passing through the hall or room. Then something happened which could not be so easily explained.

The furniture in the living room was covered with that protective plastic which makes such a distinct sound when someone sits down. Mrs. Wright was seated on the couch one evening when she heard the unmistakable squeak/squish of another person settling onto the other cushion. Indeed, the cushion and plastic covering clearly compressed under the weight. However, there was no person to be seen, only the indentation of a phantom form. Was the invisible entity of a past resident simply trying to make its presence known?

"I did get the feeling that whoever was there, just wanted us to know it's still their home, too," said Mrs. Wright, seemingly undisturbed by the incident.

One of her sons also had a bizarre sighting. One evening as he watched television, he saw a small figure running through the halls and assumed it was just his energetic little brother. The only problem with that was the fact that he remembered that his brother was not at home. In fact, no other living soul was at home, yet he was definitely not alone.

Does an old colonial family from Rockland's early days still inhabit the stone home in New City? Or, are they more recent tenants who decided that Rockland was actually a better place to be than the other-worldly alternatives?

***

An interesting side note to this story. The stone colonial in New City was not the Wright's first choice. They had wanted to buy a Victorian home in Nyack, but due to financial considerations had to pass on it.

That house happened to be on La Veta Place—the very home which was to make world-wide headlines as the first house to be declared legally haunted.

Hopefully, none of the Wright's will decide to go into real estate.

"FRO... THIS PLACE I SHALL EVER ROAM"

Most people don't equate hauntings with condos or contemporary homes—the gold standard for ghost stories are castles and stone manor houses with hidden passageways. If this is your idea of a classic haunting, then the home of Dr. Martha MacGuffie on South Mountain Road in New City is about as classic as you can get.

Dr. MacGuffie has been practicing plastic and reconstructive surgery in Rockland County for over 30 years. In addition to her skill as a surgeon, she is renowned for her humanitarian efforts with the children of Africa. As a fundraising event for her nonprofit organization, SHARE (Society for Hospital and Resource Exchange), every Halloween Dr. MacGuffie turns her home into a haunted castle with the help of local school children and cadets from West Point. However, if the ghostly tales about the house are true, it doesn't need any outside help.

Driving along the narrow twists and turns of South Mountain Road, one glimpses the rooftops and chimneys of some extraordinary homes. Taking a turn into Dr. MacGuffie's driveway, it immediately becomes evident that her home is the most extraordinary of all. Stepping out of the car is like stepping back into medieval Scotland, and indeed the stone manor house is a replica of one constructed in Scotland in the year 1299. It was built in the 1930s by Harold Deming, a naval officer and ship salvager. Mr. Deming loved his home, as well as the beautiful 31 acres of wooded hills that surrounded it. Unfortunately, he did not live much more than a decade in his beloved "castle," although some may argue that he plans to be in residence for all eternity.

Mr. Deming was buried on the estate, and his grave marker reads, "From this place I shall never roam," a statement with which many people who have been in the house would agree. Dr. MacGuffie bought the estate about 40 years ago, and the first evidence that the lord of the manor had not left his home came shortly after moving day. The housekeeper, Eliza Henry, was walking down one of the long hallways in the early morning hours of a misty day, when she suddenly saw a man standing at the opposite end looking at her. The intruder was very tall and his demeanor was stern and serious, but his most distinguishing feature was his long, straight silver hair. Before Eliza could call for help, the mysterious man vanished into thin air.

Although Eliza came from the Caribbean island of St. Kitts, she did not hold to the native beliefs in spirits. On the contrary, she was a strict Baptist and this type of experience simply did not figure into her concept of things.

She told Dr. MacGuffie about the apparent apparition and described the man in detail. Some time later, the doctor had the opportunity to speak to one of Mr. Deming's daughters, and mentioned the strange experience of her housekeeper. Upon hearing the description of the man encountered by Eliza, the daughter immediately declared, "Why, that was my father! He was six feet, six inches tall with very long, straight silver hair."

Harold Deming built his home in the style of a Scottish manor house. The hallway at the right was one place where his tall, silver-haired spirit was spotted many years after his death.

Many more indications that Mr. Deming still roams the corridors of the old stone home have presented themselves to residents, visitors and staff. Dr. MacGuffie's offices now occupy the lower level of the home, which used to contain the wine cellar and an open porch. Office manager Madeleine Blanc pointed out that closed doors are often found open. Specifically, the door to the children's examination room (which, by the way, contains an authentic secret passageway) is often found standing wide open after it has been securely shut. While drafts can be expected in such a home, it would be hard to explain how a breeze could open a closed door, and as Madeleine demonstrated, especially a door which has to be pulled open with some effort across the rough stone floor. Dr. MacGuffie has also experienced a problem with keeping doors shut. Some have even opened after being closed and locked, a problem a locksmith has been unable to resolve.

The bizarre behavior of one the doctor's cats has added a twist to the possible evidence of an unseen presence. For some reason, the cat was insisting upon going out the back door early every morning, walking along the perimeter of the property and returning to the back door, without any deviations from the course. One of Mr. Deming's daughters later revealed that this was the habit of her late father, to walk the border of his grounds every morning. Could the cat's behavior be the result of it following someone only it could see?

Then there are the sounds of footsteps in empty rooms and hallways, and that feeling that you are never alone, that someone is always watching you. Yet, despite all these classic signs of a haunting, there is no fear among those who simply say, "Oh, that must be Harold, again." Perhaps the spirit of Harold Deming does keep a silent watch upon those who occupy "his" home, and perhaps he has not created any mischief because he likes Dr. MacGuffie and how she has so tenderly preserved his beloved house and grounds.

It was probably wise that the good doctor resisted her natural surgical impulses and did not seek to cut Harold out of the house through any type of exorcism, thereby risking provoking negative or mischievous reactions. This peaceful coexistence between the living and the dead may inspire a new saying, "If the ghost ain't broken, don't fix him."

THE TORMENTED SLAVE

It must be unusual enough to work somewhere that is haunted, but can you also imagine coming home to another ghost? Such is the case of Madeleine Blanc, the office manager who shares her workspace with "Harold" in Dr. MacGuffie's Scottish-style manor house on South Mountain Road. However, while Harold appears to be a contented spirit, the presence in Madeleine's home is far from being happy.

The home, which is a converted barn, was part of the William Smith farm, also on South Mountain Road, built in 1845. While Madeleine claims that she has never sensed anything unusual there, her husband felt a definite presence in the basement. So strong were these feelings, that he would never work downstairs without leaving the door to the upstairs open. The presence was strongest in the area behind the furnace and it was always accompanied by a feeling of overwhelming sadness and the distinct impression that someone had undergone great torment and suffering. Mr. Blanc never felt threatened by the presence, but it was obviously not something with which he ever felt comfortable.

Naturally, the Blancs became curious about the history of their home and tried to find answers to the mystery of their uninvited guest. After doing some research and talking to neighbors, a story emerged which just might help explain what Mr. Blanc was experiencing. It seems that the original owner, William Smith, had two slaves, even though slavery was illegal in New York State at the time. However, whether the slaves were legal or not, it is clear that the farmer held some kind of power over them.

Smith had buried some money under the barn for safekeeping, and one day he discovered the slave Enoch (there are several variations as to the name) digging up the money in an attempt to steal it, perhaps in hopes of using it to gain his freedom. The enraged Smith threatened the worst punishment he could devise, sending Enoch back down South into a very brutal and very legal slavery system. Terrified by the threat, Enoch's tormented mind came to the conclusion that returning to the South would be a fate worse than death. In a final act of a desperate man, he hung himself in the barn. The slave's suicide occurred in the area that today would be behind the furnace, the exact site where Mr. Blanc felt the deepest grief and torment.

Did the strong emotions of this terrible event leave some kind of impression on the site, or is the slave's ghost locked for all eternity to that spot? If Enoch's tortured soul does still hang in limbo in the basement of this converted barn, it is a true tragedy that he has yet to experience what he most desired: freedom.

DARK SHADOWS IN THE MANSION

The typical home in Pearl River is a modest Cape Cod with just enough property to have a lawn on which the kids can play. It's therefore hard to imagine that Pearl River also has an extravagant stone mansion with a lawn large enough for hundreds of people to play—18 holes, that is.

The spectacular Mansion at Blue Hill restaurant with is rolling green golf course is anything but typical by any town's standards. Built in 1900 by Montgomery Maze, the rough stone walls stand in sharp contrast to the interior's finely carved mahogany and Tiffany stained glass. Anyone should have felt extremely fortunate to be able to call such a place home, but to have a mansion like this just as a summer home, seems to be almost too much luck for one person. However, as this sprawling mansion was built with only two fireplaces, it would have been too cold during the winter months and was actually used simply as a warm-weather "party house."

Ninety-eight years later, the spirit of the place is basically the same, only now the parties are catered affairs at the Mansion's restaurant, and the stables no longer house horses, but golf carts. In a county of rampant over-development, a visit to this tranquil mansion on the hill above the lake, surrounded by trees and lush grass, gives one the opportunity to take a deep breath and enjoy the beautiful vistas. Dinner and a round of golf aren't bad ideas, either. With so much to offer, it isn't surprising that the spirit of the place remains intact. In fact, there may be more spirit there than one would imagine…

This c.1900 photo of the original Maze mansion still
hangs on the walls of the former private estate.
One of the former residents may also still be hanging around.

The manager of the Mansion's restaurant, Jean, is quite candid about the haunting, "Sure there's a ghost. Many people have seen him, but he's very friendly and doesn't bother anyone." Jean went on to explain that on several occasions, employees have seen a dark, shadowy figure pass by, only to turn and find no one there. The chef, who works in a kitchen which is in an original part of the house, has seen this dark figure many times, times when he has been the only living person in the place.

"At first I didn't think there was any truth to these stories," Jean explained, "until one morning when I was here early and saw out of the corner of my eye a figure pass by me in the hall. I thought it was one of the waitresses and called her name. There was no reply. I searched the place and found that I was the only one here."

Such incidents have occurred on a regular basis over the last nine years Jean has worked there. In fact, the morning of the interview, Jean had opened the restaurant and was alone as she began to work. She went into the kitchen for a moment and when she returned, there was an open bottle of water next to her work. "It wasn't there before. I guess he just wants to let me know he's here."

Who is "he"? Well, the question is open to debate, but the general feeling is that the spirit is that of Robert Montgomery Maze, the original owner's grandson who may have died in the house. A psychic who visited the Mansion claimed that she had seen a young man holding a book going into Jean's second-floor office at the top of the stairs. Indeed, the room had been a library in Robert's time, and perhaps he is using his eternal rest to finally catch up on his reading?

Robert may not be the only spirit that walks the corridors of the Mansion, opening and closing doors, or starting appliances when no one is around. When Jean had been working at the restaurant for about a year she experienced and unfortunate accident, or so it must have read on the insurance forms.

"I was finishing up the night's business when the heavy door of the safe slammed onto my thumb." Without elaborating on the gruesome details, her thumb required surgery and still bothers her to this day. The safe was very large, and the heavy door could not have closed due to a draft, or even a strong wind, in the unlikely event that one had been present inside the restaurant at the time.

The accident had remained a mystery until the psychic reported that there was also a ghost of a young woman present. Apparently Robert's girlfriend during his lifetime, Beatrice, had pushed the door closed out of jealousy toward what she viewed as a potential rival for Robert's affections. The psychic also said that Robert would make certain that no harm would ever befall Jean again, and for the past eight years there have been no further accidents.

Was this angry woman ghost truly the spirit of Robert's deceased girlfriend, come back to join him? Or is she the result of something more sinister? There is a story of a murder that had been committed on the property generations ago, the murder of a young woman. Her body had been discovered floating in a pond, and the crime was never solved. It is not uncommon to experience ghostly phenomena at the site of a murder, and where there is one ghost, there are often others.

While it is clear that Jean is relatively unperturbed by all these otherworldly occurrences, not all of the employees have been on friendly terms with the unseen guests. Apparently, the previous manager was not in

Robert's good graces, and would occasionally do things that annoyed the deceased ex-resident. "When Robert was really angry, he would turn the glass on the wall sconces," Jean explained. "The manager would come in early in the morning and find them all backwards."

These sconces line the walls of the main dining rooms. They have a brass base and the glass consists of layers of frosted leaves. Upon testing how easy it was to spin the glass, it was found that they wouldn't budge. If an employee had been trying to play a joke on his boss, it would have taken considerable time and effort—time he probably would not have had without being seen by someone else.

On another occasion, an employee who had opened up the restaurant and thought he was alone went upstairs to a second-floor office. After a few minutes he clearly heard footsteps down on the first floor. As no one else was scheduled to be in at such an early hour, he went to investigate. When he descended the stairs to the main dining rooms, he noticed that the sections of the tablecloths that hung down had all been flipped up onto the tops of the tables.

The Mansion restaurant as it appears today, and one of the glass wall sconces that are the targets of ghostly pranks.

He called out, asking who was there, but got no response. A search revealed no one. Determined to uncover the prankster, he went out the front door in an attempt to identify the footprints of the guilty party. There had been several inches of snow that night, and his footprints were clearly visible leading from his car and up the stairs, but there was only one set of tracks. No human being could possibly have entered and exited the Mansion without having his feet leave a trace that morning. Unless, of course, he had no human feet with which to leave tracks.

Visitors who have not heard a word about the ghosts have also reported strange experiences. A telephone repairman was working in the basement one day, and when he came upstairs he rather abruptly informed Jean, "You know you have a ghost in this place." He didn't care to elaborate, nor did he care to stick around once the job was done.

"Personally, I like having Elmer around," Jeans says rather matter-of-factly, given the circumstances. "Elmer is just the name I gave the ghost, and the psychic said he likes it. We get along just fine. He's a part of this place, he has a right to be here."

Whether it is Elmer, Robert, Beatrice, a murder victim, or whoever or whatever is at the root of this haunting, the facts remain the same. Something inexplicable by ordinary standards occurs frequently at the Mansion at Blue Hill.

How do the owners feel about this haunted property? Probably not the way you might think. You see, the Mansion is one of two restaurants they own. The other is in a 19th century structure in Bergen County, and it is much more haunted than the Mansion, but that's another story...

STILL AT HOME

If hauntings are the result of some tragic or traumatic human experience, then one would expect older homes to have a higher percentage of ghosts, as there has been more opportunity to create a haunting. In Rockland County, many of the oldest homes are the charming Dutch colonials that once sat isolated amongst acres of farmland and forest. Do these structures, which have seen over two hundred years of human drama, actually have a high percentage of unexplained events?

Statistics say yes. Including the following story, at least six other hauntings in Rockland involve old Dutch colonials. So as appealing as one of these beautiful homes with their stone walls and angled roofs appear, remember that the history of a place is not always happy, and some ghostly residents do not want strangers in *their* home.

Several decades ago, a woman moved into one of Rockland's architectural treasures, the Dutch colonial. The house was on a lovely corner property in northern Spring Valley and seemed miles, and generations, away from the growing traffic and congestion of the county. It seemed to be the ideal place, except for the fact that the woman never felt quite alone. And whatever or whoever the presence was, it was not happy.

One day when the feeling was particularly strong, the woman was walking across an unobstructed area of the living room when something tripped her. It was real, it was solid, but whatever it was, was quite invisible. On several other occasions while going downstairs or across a room some unseen force tried to trip up her legs as if attempting to make her fall.

Strange events were not restricted to the inside of the house. One afternoon as she was tending to her garden, she saw an older woman in turn-of-the-century clothing and a young man in what appeared to be a World War I uniform. The pair walked along casually as if they owned the place, and then disappeared. Several months later, the woman was talking to a neighbor who had lived in the area her entire life. The neighbor mentioned that she had a picture of some former residents of the woman's home. Later, when she brought over the picture of a mother with her soldier son, the owner of the Dutch colonial saw that the figures in the picture were exactly the same as those she had seen from her garden that day. The spirits had, in fact, actually once owned the place.

On another occasion, the woman was reading in her parlor when two small dogs, a poodle and a Pomeranian, came trotting into the room, stopped and looked right at her. This presented several problems. The woman did not own any dogs, and no doors had been left open to let the animals inside. The most difficult thing to explain, however, was when the two dogs simply vanished into thin air. A few days later while working in her yard, she was clearing some brush when she came across two weathered stone grave markers—grave markers for a pair of dogs. Were they the graves of former beloved pets, and do their spirits still roam the house waiting to hear their master's voice?

As difficult as it is to comprehend the nature of a ghost in human form, animal ghosts seem even more bizarre. However, there has been at least one other report of an animal apparition in the county—a contractor renovating a Piermont home watched as a cat entered the room, stared at him with classic feline intensity, and then vanished right before his eyes.

Is this Dutch colonial in Spring Valley still visited by former residents and their pets? Perhaps more evidence could be gathered if the current owners were questioned, but how does one approach strangers and ask if their home has any World War I soldiers or disappearing poodles?

THE MOST HAUNTED HOUSE IN ROCKLAND

"Pam and Edward Dodge" lived in New York City until they experienced a terrifying break-in by a drug-crazed man. They then decided it was time to move their family to Rockland County for peace and quiet, into a home where they would be safe from intruders. Unfortunately, they would find no peace, and their new home just might have more "intruders" than any other house in Rockland.

At first, everything seemed to be ideal; they purchased a beautiful 18th century farmhouse in West Nyack, and the Dodge's and their two young children looked forward to the start of their new lives in the "burbs." Yet within just a few weeks of moving into the house, Edward began exhibiting an unpleasant change in his behavior. Of course, this could be considered normal in lieu of the stress involved in buying a house and undergoing a complete change of lifestyle.

However, these altered moods were also accompanied by what appeared at first to be a minor, yet persistent physical ailment. Edward decided to consult a physician who put him through a battery of tests. The reports came back conclusive and devastating. After only three months in their new home, Edward was diagnosed with a fatal illness. Everything medically possible was done, but he died within a year, leaving his young widow and children grief-stricken and alone. Or so it seemed at first.

Pam's overwhelming sorrow found momentary respite when she began to feel Edward's presence in the house. Rather than being frightened by the presence, she felt comforted and would hold long conversations with her departed husband. At times she tried to convince herself it was all in her imagination, that no one could communicate with the dead, but then something occurred which her own eyes told her was not in her imagination.

Unable to sleep late one night, Pam decided that instead of tossing and turning, she would get up and do some of the laundry that her kids were so adept at creating. A couple of hours later, with a basket of clean clothes under one arm and a cup of coffee in the other hand, she turned to leave the laundry room after her late night chore was complete. There in the doorway, blocking her exit, was a white, cloud-like form. It was at least seven feet tall and a yard wide, and was totally transparent. Pam did not feel afraid, but she knew this presence was not her husband and her first thought was for her children's safety.

Speaking to the wispy entity, she said that she didn't care who it was or why it was there. All that she asked was that if it insisted on appearing, that it appear only to her and that it should never frighten her children. Having thus spoken her mind, the entity suddenly vanished and the rest of the night passed without incident. Obviously not wanting to alarm her son and daughter, she did not mention the apparition in the laundry room and hoped that nothing more would happen. But like everything else that had occurred since moving into the old house, events would be beyond her control.

There was some period of quiet, but then one day the children told their mother that faces were peering at them through the darkness of their upstairs bedroom. They described these faces as being those of young children with straight black hair and sad eyes, and they would appear right next to the bed and just silently stare. Naturally, they were frightened by the presence of

44

these disembodied eyes and heads, but Pam tried to assure them it was all in their imagination, an assurance she did not fully believe herself.

Pam's cousin, Bill, came to spend some time with her after he recovered from his own serious, life-threatening illness. Bill slept on the living room couch and was awakened late one night to see two dark forms floating near the television. The television was not on, and the forms could not have been shadows as they were not flat against the wall. They were clearly floating in the middle of the room.

Bill rubbed his eyes and searched the room for a plausible explanation, but the two dark forms simply disappeared leaving no clues as to their origin or why they had appeared. In the following days, Bill was also to find that one door was frequently standing wide open, even after he had closed it himself several times. There was also a presence, or several presences, throughout the house. They were tangible, yet difficult to describe, other then they generated the distinct feeling that someone or something was in the room with him.

Pam's mother also had some strange experiences, as did other family members and guests when they visited the beautiful, but mysterious, old farmhouse. After years of these bizarre and inexplicable occurrences, Pam finally decided it was time to get help. But where does one go in Rockland County for such a problem? While discussing the situation with a friend, he told Pam about a recent article that had appeared in the *Journal News*, written by Nancy Cacioppo. The article was about this author's search for Rockland ghost stories, and to shorten a long series of events and phone messages, we arranged a little exploratory mission.

On an early spring afternoon in 1998, Nancy Cacioppo and I went to Pam's house. Meeting us there were local psychics Lawrence Hoff and Martha Piesco Hoff. For the next several hours, the Hoff's took a spiritual tour of the home. They were to return a month later with half a dozen of their students, and the following is a compilation of those two visits. (It should be noted that no one was briefed beforehand about any of the previous encounters, and many of the psychics described the same things although they worked separately without consulting one another on their findings until the session was complete.)

The house was built along an old crossroads, and a Revolutionary War era sentry still walks the front porch keeping an eye on all who come and go. In the living room (where Bill saw the two dark forms), there is a mother and her young daughter dressed in colonial-style clothing. They had suffered some kind of loss and frequently pass into the living room through the door that mysteriously opens by itself, and wait for the return of someone long gone.

In the parlor to the right of the front door, was discovered a strong "energy vortex" going deep into the ground. Pam explained that directly under that spot in the basement was the site of the old well. Down a hallway from this room in a bathroom is a heavy, overwhelming feeling of sadness, grief and the sense of drowning—a feeling some found too strong for comfort. It was in this hallway that Pam first encountered the towering, cloud-like entity.

The basement was also a place of great sadness and suffering. Sick and wounded Revolutionary era soldiers (British and their mercenaries) hid from local patriots in this cellar, enduring many hardships and much pain. Several died there. Their spirits still gather near the old stove, waiting for relief from their suffering.

Upstairs in a small room, a mother gave birth to a child who lived only briefly. Sounds of a baby crying have been heard coming from that room. In the room next to it, where Pam's children sleep, there are the spirits of several young Indian boys and girls. This is where Pam's children claimed to have seen the faces with the straight black hair and sad eyes. The psychics felt that hundreds of years ago, a group of adult Indians died or were killed by these grounds, their bodies buried in a mass grave on the spot where the house now stands. The spirits of the Indian children still search for their missing parents, each night their sad eyes looking out across centuries of loneliness.

There is another small room where strange sounds are heard, and where one gets the skin-crawling sense of being trapped or imprisoned. And then there is the kind, loving spirit of Edward Dodge, present in every room in the house, tenderly looking after his beloved wife and children, from whom not even death could separate him.

Has the accumulated grief of generations of human suffering left its imprint in the very walls of this old farmhouse, emotional imprints that hang like psychic paintings to be viewed by those who are sensitive and empathetic? Or perhaps something even deeper and stronger is happening here. Many reported hauntings have been found to be connected to deep wells or natural springs, and it has been suggested that these openings into the earth create some type of energetic force that draws spiritual energy like a magnet. If the old well under Pam's farmhouse does exert a strange, otherworldly force, has it actually spawned tragedy in the lives of those who have lived there, lives that remain connected to the site even after death?

Some may argue that it is merely an old house that has seen more than its share of the human condition, and that its age and history encourages the imagination to flights of fancy. To be sure, there is no hard scientific proof to this group haunting, yet the fact that many people have had identical experiences and feelings in the various rooms of that house must shake the confidence of the most steadfast skeptic.

Taking all of this into consideration, this old farmhouse has justly earned the title of The Most Haunted House in Rockland.

Book Two

BLOODY NIGHT

When "Ann Fidallo" and her husband bought their 18th Century home in the northwest corner of Rockland County, they were proud to own a place with so much history. Unfortunately, they were to find out one bloody night that some history is better left in the past.

Soon after moving in, the couple began hearing inexplicable sounds, such as footsteps when no one could be seen. While her husband always dismissed these events, Ann was becoming increasingly uncomfortable. There was clearly at least one unearthly presence, and she knew it was neither happy nor friendly.

While making some inquiries about the history of their home, the Fidallo's learned that in colonial times the house had been along the main route through the Ramapo Mountains. During the Revolution, both armies had passed by, and both may have used the place to care for their wounded and sick. Ann soon had her suspicions that at least one poor soul in the house did not recover, nor did he ever leave.

The couple was sound asleep one night when Ann suddenly awoke from a nightmare. She had the sense that something was terribly wrong. Shifting her body to turn and face her husband, she realized that the sheets were soaking wet. Pulling her hand out from under the blankets, she turned on the light and saw that her fingers were dripping with blood. Shaking her husband awake, they threw back the covers to find that both of his legs were drenched in blood.

Even though a dangerous amount of blood had obviously been lost, Mr. Fidallo did not feel lightheaded, or in any way uncomfortable, except for the fear that naturally would accompany such a sight. The couple frantically wiped away the blood, searching for the severe injury that must have caused such profuse blood loss. However, even after all the blood had been washed away, not even the tiniest pinprick could be found. Mr. Fidallo's legs and the sheets had been soaked in a life-threatening amount of fresh blood, but it could not have come from Mr. Fidallo, and it certainly did not come from Ann. So what was its source?

They may never know for certain, but Ann believes that it was some kind of manifestation from the wounded Revolutionary soldier who died there. Perhaps his legs had been horribly maimed, and he needed to get that message of his suffering known. Were such bloody occurrences to be commonplace at the Fidallo home? The former unbeliever and his wife did stay long enough to find out.

SUNSET SCREAM

Every high school has its terrifying legends, tall tales that are usually short on facts. For instance, an infamous path through the woods where students disappear, or an annual dance from which one unlucky participant will never return alive. Such stories are usually designed to frighten freshmen or to make girlfriends cuddle up a little closer, and they have little or no basis in reality.

In the 1950s, one Rockland high school circulated a classic cemetery legend. It involved the Old Brick Church in Spring Valley, and the story claimed that every night a phantom, blood-curdling scream would pierce the air just as the sun set. Conveniently, the legend also claimed that the scream would best be heard if a 15-year-old girl was present. A tale like that afforded the perfect opportunity for a group of high school girls to dare one another into tempting fate in the fading light of the cemetery one evening in 1952.

Kathleen M. recalls, "Only one of us had a car, so we decided to see how many of us could fit. We managed to squeeze in ten or twelve girls (cars were considerably more spacious then) and headed for the church."

The Old Brick Church.

The group definitely acted more like they were on their way to a party than a ghost hunt. Even after arriving at the cemetery, the joking and laughing continued. This adolescent playfulness might have lasted well into the darkness, had it not been for what occurred as the sun slipped beneath the horizon.

"We had almost forgotten why we were there. Suddenly, just at the moment that the sun set, there was the loud and terrifying scream of a young girl. It gave me goose bumps and made the hairs stand up on the back of my neck. We stood in stunned silence for a second, looking at one another to see if it could have been one of our group playing a joke. It was clear that the scream could not have come from any of us, and this was definitely no joke. We all ran for our lives and I was surprised that nobody was trampled in the panic. We piled into the car and sped away as fast as we could."

Even though time passed, Kathleen was still haunted by that frightening day in the cemetery. Forty-three years later, she mentioned the episode to her friend, Alice. Oddly, Alice was not surprised by the story. It seems that when Alice was a little girl, she used to accompany her grandmother to the cemetery to tend to the grave of a relative. Each time they visited, her grandmother would warn her not to go to the cemetery alone, and never, never go at night, because a horrible tragedy had occurred there. The ominous warning was etched deeply into her mind, especially after she heard the reason behind it.

Alice's grandmother told her the story of a 15-year-old local girl who had been abducted from her home. The kidnapper brought his terrified victim to the cemetery behind the Brick Church, where she was brutally murdered. The girl screamed at the moment of her death, the last seconds of life ebbing away just as the dying rays of sunlight passed beneath the horizon. Her body was discovered the next day behind the church—her murderer was never found.

When Kathleen heard the story of the murdered girl she was determined to return to the cemetery again, even though more than four decades had passed since her first encounter. Alice agreed to accompany her and to bring along her 15-year-old daughter. As the trio of women stood anxiously behind the church in the fading daylight, they thought they could hear voices in the distance. No one was visible, and no words could be understood, but still the voices seemed to be coming from somewhere.

Then a car appeared. It was an old green Packard in excellent condition with shiny, spoked wheels—the type of car that would have been in use at the time of the girl's murder. The car drove slowly through the cemetery and went behind some bushes. It never emerged from the other side of the bushes, and the women could not understand how the car could possibly have gone without them seeing it leave.

However, their preoccupation with the old Packard and the distant voices ended abruptly at sunset. It was then that the terrified scream of a dying 15-year-old girl rent the air, sending waves of fear through the women. Like a repeat of the scene in 1952, the women ran to their car and sped away.

Several weeks passed as Kathleen and Alice discussed what they should do next. As this was obviously not something they could simply forget, they decided to try to capture some hard evidence of this haunting. They returned with cameras and a tape recorder, determined to get proof that these weren't just figments of their imaginations.

The two women waited with anticipation for the sun to set, cameras ready, hearts pounding. However, as the last golden-orange rays of light were extinguished, there was complete silence. They waited and waited, but no screams could be heard. Perhaps the restless spirit had chosen not to make her presence known that night, or perhaps the lack of ghostly phenomena was the result of the fact that they had neglected to bring a 15-year-old girl, an apparently essential component to experiencing the phantom scream.

Had the scream Kathleen heard actually been part of a teenager's prank in 1952? Was the scream that she, Alice and her daughter heard again in 1995 just the result of the power of suggestion? These doubts must have filled Kathleen's mind, until a few weeks later when she decided to listen to the tape. At the point on the tape that corresponded to the time of sunset, a girl's scream had been recorded!

Incredulous at first, Kathleen rewound the tape and played it again and again. Neither she nor Alice had heard a sound while they were in the cemetery, but the tape recorder had clearly captured the murdered girl's tormented scream.

Witnesses claim the murdered girl's scream can be heard at sunset.

Naturally, when Kathleen related her story to me, I was intrigued—intrigued to the point where I knew I had to visit the old murder scene. While I didn't know any teenage girls who would be willing to go along, I did have a very willing partner in my boyfriend, Bob Strong.

We decided to take our field trip on the spur of the moment one Saturday evening in the late autumn of 1998. The sun was already low in the sky, so as Bob drove, I loaded the camera, tape recorder and camcorder. We arrived at the cemetery about 15 minutes before sunset and set up all the equipment. As darkness approached, the temperature dropped rapidly and a biting wind whipped across the exposed hill upon which the beautiful old church stands. This turn in the weather was certainly no surprise—I don't know if I have ever been to a cemetery that was not cold and windy.

As we awaited sunset, I noticed how the area had changed over the years. Like the rest of Rockland, new houses had sprung up everywhere. There were clearly voices to be heard, as well as children screaming and dogs barking, but the sources of all the noises were plain to see racing around in the backyards of the homes now bordering the cemetery. As I paced back and forth trying to keep warm, I thought that if the ghost of the murdered girl was going to scream, she was going to have to make it a loud one to be heard.

The orb of the sun started to be consumed by the horizon, and I stopped my pacing. Bob and I stood silently, cameras ready, tape recorder and camcorder running. Half the sun disappeared. Then just an arced sliver of light remained, and seconds later, like a switch being turned off, the last rays of sunlight disappeared.

Nothing. No ghostly sounds. No antique automobiles. Not a single disembodied voice. We waited a few more minutes. Still nothing. Finally, my numbed toes and fingers signaled retreat. Not unlike the actions of people who had heard a ghost, we grabbed our equipment and rushed to the car, not to speed away, but to turn on the heat.

Disappointed, but still hopeful, we reviewed both the videotape and audiotape when we got home. Unfortunately, there was nothing to be seen but the images of two very cold, but alive, people, and nothing to be heard but the sound of the wind rushing over the microphone. It would have been nice to be able to report something a little more dramatic than the onset of hypothermia, but such is the nature of ghost hunting.

Is the spirit of a young girl, murdered a generation ago, trapped at the scene of her untimely death? Can her phantom scream be heard in the cemetery only by girls the same age as she was when she died? Is the ghost of her murderer also trapped in the cemetery, doomed for all eternity to drive his green car past the scene of his horrible deed?

Perhaps some high school legends should be believed.

***

Within a year after this story appeared in the first edition of *Haunted Hudson Valley*, several people contacted me and said they have heard the scream at sunset. They also claim to have recorded other strange sounds and felt more than one presence. Maybe the Old Brick Church cemetery has more than one tale to tell.

GRAVE MARKS

Everyone knows that by staying in shape, you might just be able to postpone that inevitable trip to the grave. However, for Rockland County resident Barry Marks, staying in shape brought a most unusual trip *to* the grave.

Jogging through the woods with your dog is a great way to exercise and unwind. All the tensions of life seem to disappear in the serene atmosphere, or so Barry thought until his dog began barking for no apparent reason. The Doberman usually remained faithfully at his side, but when he passed by a particular area behind North Rockland High School, the dog would run to one spot and start barking with extreme agitation. After calling and whistling for him, he would return, but each time the same thing would happen at the same exact spot.

Finally one day, Barry followed his dog to see what could possibly be upsetting him, and ended up getting a little upset himself. To his surprise, the spot to which the dog kept running was actually a small cemetery behind the tennis courts. Most of the old stones were severely damaged, except for the ones that his dog was staring at barking. Barry began staring, too, when he realized the family name on the stones. They were the graves of Jacob and his wife, and their last name was Marks, the same as Barry's last name!

To further the bizarre "coincidence," one of the dates of death, February 4, 1846, was *exactly* 100 years to the day of Barry's birth on February 4, 1946! One can not even begin to calculate the odds of finding a grave marker with the same last name with such a date, let alone begin to fathom why his dog would run over to it and bark.

Is there some kind of family connection that Barry's ancestors were trying to make, some kind of message they needed to pass on from beyond the grave? Did they watch every day as he jogged by, trying to get his attention? Are there truly ghosts here, forever trapped in this cemetery; entities that only the keen senses of a dog could detect?

Perhaps this was all an amazing coincidence, but the next time Barry Marks' dog is barking, maybe he should just keep on running.

One of the Marks' grave stones.

UNTIL DEATH DO THEY PART

The day a couple gets married is supposed to be the happiest day of their lives. In reality, it is often a very stressful day that the couple and their guests are just happy to survive. Unfortunately, there are instances when some guests actually do not survive. Occasionally, older relatives or friends can overdo the celebrating: eating, drinking and dancing more than their hearts can bear. The death of a loved one at a wedding reception is extremely traumatic for all concerned (and more common than you might think!), and may be especially traumatic for the spirit of the one whose untimely demise may hold them to that spot for eternity.

A popular location for wedding receptions and other events is the Colonial Inn in Norwood, New Jersey. Owned by the same family that owns the "hauntingly" beautiful Mansion restaurant in Pearl River, the Colonial Inn also seems to have its share of otherworldly guests. As with many sites of unusual activities, this property has legends about its past.

There are stories about it being a Revolutionary War-era burial site. During the Civil War, part of the original structure may have been a prison. During Prohibition, there were rumors that there was an underground distillery with tunnels that led to other buildings, tunnels offering not only escape routes for the bootleggers, but clandestine routes for moving their valuable "product." In the 1930s, the building became a legitimate restaurant, which for many years was known as Widner's.

So by the time the building became the Colonial Inn, the location may already have had the shadowy imprints of fallen soldiers, despairing prisoners and violent gangsters. However, even if all those stories proved to have no basis in truth, enough has happened in modern times to add strength to the alleged cases of hauntings.

I went to the Colonial Inn one day in January of 1999 to meet with the manager, and we sat in his office discussing the strange goings on. He began by telling me about Agnes, an older woman who died of a heart attack in one of the reception rooms in 1984. Odd things seemed to begin happening in the days following the woman's death, things attributed to her wandering spirit. The manager did make it clear, however, that it soon became common practice for the staff to blame Agnes for anything and everything that happened.

Yet even with these lighthearted exaggerations of mishaps, some things clearly lacked human explanations. Objects on shelves would suddenly fall to the floor. A dark shape would move across the security monitors in areas that contained no living beings. Then there were the sounds.

Late one evening, as the manager worked in his downstairs office (there are three levels at the Inn), he heard a door slam very loudly up on the main level. Generally, he would pay no attention to such a sound. However, since he had personally locked the doors after the rest of the staff had gone, supposedly leaving him alone in the building, the slamming door created enough concern for him to call the police. Obviously, the manager believed it was a human intruder, but after he and the police carefully searched every square inch of the facility, his thoughts turned to Agnes.

Not all inexplicable events occur in the dead of night. One afternoon, the manager was working in an upper level office, again, all alone. Or so he thought. He began to hear voices coming from somewhere on that floor. After repeated searches, he tried to chalk it up to his imagination, but the voices persisted, although he could not make out what they were saying. Then, one female voice suddenly became all too clear as it whispered his name directly into his ear! Turning quickly, he found no one. The manager freely admitted that the event "gave him the creeps," to put it mildly.

Other employees have also heard voices from the upper level, voices loud enough to be heard down on the main floor. Is Agnes trying to deliver a message from the grave, or is she simply having "conversations" with other spirits that walk the halls of the Colonial Inn? The facility has been the scene of two other victims of heart attacks over the years. While modern technology kept them artificially alive as they were rushed to a local hospital, there may be some evidence that while their bodies were taken away, their spirits remained at the scene of the party.

As the Inn has many rooms and halls, I asked the manager to tell me in which rooms the heart attacks had occurred, but requested that he not tell me where in the rooms they happened. Our first stop was a room on the lower level, and after taking a few photos, I switched on my EMF meter and began to slowly walk back and forth across the floor. Readings remained at normal levels, until I passed an area where the dance floor met the carpet.

The increase was small, borderline for the unnatural realm, but an increase which I was able to confirm with readings obtained by leaving the area and returning several times. As I concentrated on this small area (roughly a five-foot long oval), my back was turned to the manager standing in the doorway. As I looked over my shoulder to ask if that spot had any significance, his jaw-dropping expression gave me the answer. In that huge room, I had found the few square feet where Agnes had fallen and breathed her last.

Slightly unnerved myself, we proceeded upstairs to the main catering hall—a beautiful room full of natural light spilling in from tall windows. Again, I began the process of scanning the room for any signs of high EMF readings. Once again, I hit an unusual spot on the dance floor, only this time the readings shot up. In addition, much to my dismay, there was also an uneasy coldness about the area. The spot had a definite outline, the meter returning to normal levels just a few inches away from its border. To put it plainly, the area roughly correlated to the size of a prone human figure. Looking to the manager as I stood above the spot, I simply asked, "Here?"

Somewhat surprised, he did confirm that the spot had been where the most recent heart attack victim had fallen. He quickly went on to add that paramedics had responded immediately, and had put the man on life support. He and the staff had always assumed that the man had not actually died there on the dance floor. Circumstances may call for a reevaluation of that assumption.

It should be noted that out of the literally thousands of receptions and parties that have taken place at the Colonial Inn over the decades, only three unfortunate occurrences isn't bad. Many people in Bergen and Rockland Counties have spent countless happy hours there celebrating with family and friends, with the scariest thing encountered being those plaid pants your uncle was wearing. I personally have attended at least two wedding receptions and a bowling awards dinner (yes, I did receive a trophy) in the very room where Agnes died, and never noticed anything unusual.

Perhaps during those times when the place is filled with people, music and laughter, the spirits are content. It may only be when the party is over, the people have gone home and silence has descended, that the ghosts are filled with discontent and strive to make their presence known to a world they left so abruptly. Perhaps that line in the marriage vows should be amended, that not even unto death do they depart...

The ballroom at the Colonial Inn where
Agnes' energy might still be detected.

JUST PASSING BY

"Cynthia" did not believe in ghosts, at least not until one dark winter's night near an old cemetery. There were some patches of ice as she drove along Sickletown Road from New City to West Nyack, so she slowed down. Paying careful attention to the road, Cynthia noticed that someone had pulled over up ahead, and she slowed down even more, thinking that there may have been an accident.

However, before reaching the other car, she saw something that made her stop, too, and it wasn't ice. It wasn't even on the road, it was *above* it. In the trees at the edge of the other side of the road, there was a fog-like mass, roughly the size of a person. Fog in such frigid conditions was unusual enough, but adding to it that this fog *moved*, made it all the more bizarre. This is not to say that it simply blew away in the wind—it moved in what seemed to be a self-determined way, regardless of any wind.

Cynthia took her eyes away for a second to look at the man who had pulled his car off the road. He had gotten out, and was standing and staring at this unusual mist. She wanted to go over and ask the man what he thought it was, but just then the cloudy shape began moving onto the road. Slowly, silently, it continued its movement, seemingly determined to reach some destination. It did not have to go far. By the combined light of the car headlights, Cynthia and the man watched as the mist-like form glided across the road and entered the gates of what she quickly realized was an old cemetery. That was enough for her. Removing her foot from the break, she hit the accelerator and drove away.

As she began to get some distance between herself and the traveling apparition, she thought several times about turning around and talking to the man who had been as transfixed as she had been. However, Cynthia finally decided that her nerves had been strained enough for one night and continued on home.

Was the Sickletown Cemetery ghost simply the result of an unusual combination of atmospheric conditions? Could it have been the headlights playing off the moisture in the air? Perhaps, but it is quite a coincidence that this atmospheric aberration headed right into an old abode of the dead. For the brave or simply curious who have nothing to do some cold, dark night, this may be the perfect opportunity to discover if when we pass on, do we still occasionally come back to pass on by?

***

About a year after this story was published, a man who grew up near the cemetery told me that early in the 20th Century, a young boy had a rope tied to a high branch of a tree in the cemetery, and would swing on the rope out over a stream and jump in.

Unfortunately, one day he fell off the rope before reaching the water and was killed by the impact with the hard ground. Many people claim that his spirit still walks the grounds of the old Sickletown Cemetery, but at least he may not be alone…

The gate to the Sickletown Cemetery. A plaque on the pillar commemorates the burial of 18 Revolutionary War soldiers there.

A GOOD EVENING AT THE LOCUST TREE INN

Along the main street in the college town of New Paltz, it's not hard to distinguish the students (on foot, wearing baggy clothes and having multiple body-piercings) from local residents (those in cars desperately looking for parking spaces). Housing is also at a premium these days as a growing number students continue to stream into town every fall, only to be gone in the spring. However, there may be at least one resident who has no plans to move. In fact, she may still be in the same house where she lived over two hundred years ago.

A short distance from the hustle and bustle of the downtown is another world, an old world that dates back a century before the United States was even a country. Strolling along Huguenot Street (which holds the title of America's oldest street) one passes a series of small stone houses that each have about three hundred years of stories to tell. It is a peaceful street, an ancient oasis in an often overwhelming modern world. In the midst of this oasis is a beautiful "new" house, a colonial that "only" dates back to 1759, with a large 1847 addition. The original stone structure was built by Abraham Elting, and the property remained in the Elting family until 1954.

The farmland surrounding the house came to be known as the Locust Tree Farm (due, of course, to the numerous locust trees on the property). When the house and property came into the hands of Joanne and Gordon Kreth in the 1970s, the land was transformed into a golf course and the house became the Locust Tree Inn restaurant. Several years ago, the restaurant was purchased by Karen and Joseph Fitzgerald, and today it continues to be one of the finest dining locations in the Hudson Valley.

The Locust Tree Inn.

With so many changes taking place over the years, it's comforting to know that some things don't change. For instance, at least one of the original occupants of the house may still be there. While none of the owners ever experienced anything unusual, members of the staff and guests have heard a woman's footsteps, seen a shadowy figure and sensed a female presence in the upstairs portion of the house. Some even claim to have sensed two distinct female spirits.

It would be easy to dismiss such things as the result of one too many cocktails with dinner. However, that can't explain such things as the dog (who definitely had not been drinking) who became extremely agitated in the upstairs hallway, and paced nervously while staring at what appeared to human eyes to be a blank section of wall.

Perhaps one of the most bizarre occurrences involved two couples dining at the Inn one evening. Unaware of the rumors of a haunting, the two ladies excused themselves from the table to use the bathrooms on the second floor. Curiosity about the old house compelled them to take a peek at some of the other rooms upstairs. Opening the door to an old bedroom that served as a storage room for decorations and odds and ends, the two women stepped inside. There was no one else in the room at the time. In fact, the entire second floor was vacant except for the two ladies.

However, the lack of another human presence did not seem to hamper the disembodied voice that suddenly said, "Good evening, Denise!" As one of the women's names was Denise, this made the experience all the more unnerving and they ran back downstairs visibly shaken. Yet, in their fear and confusion, could they have misunderstood the name spoken by the mysterious voice?

Some believe that one of the spirits that still roam the Locust Tree Inn is that of the wife of the original builder, Abraham Elting. Mrs. Elting's maiden name was DuBois, and her first name was Dina. Perhaps one of the women guests that night had been mistaken for Mrs. Elting. Perhaps another spirit resident of the house was simply trying to greet her old friend by saying, "Good evening, Dina!"

If Mrs. Elting or any other past residents do still walk the halls of their beloved home, one cannot blame them. It is a beautiful place that is lovingly maintained. And if you do decide to dine at the Locust Tree Inn, regardless of whether or not you encounter a ghost, you will be guaranteed of having a good evening.

THE OLDEST HAUNTED STREET IN AMERICA

One would think that if any place in the country is haunted, it would be on the Oldest Street in America (Huguenot Street in New Paltz, see previous story). Indeed, in addition to the strange events at the Locust Tree Inn, Huguenot Street has at least three more ghosts that might also make the road eligible for the title of the Oldest Haunted Street in America.

At the old stone Abraham Hasbrouck House, the specter of a man in colonial-style clothing has been seen on the property. Witnesses say that the man is carrying an ax on his shoulder and is followed by his ever-faithful ghostly dog. They appear as if they are returning from some chore, and they both enter the house. Whether they enter through the door, or actually *through* the door isn't clear, but it is clear that neither of them is an earthly human or dog.

Nearby in the DuBois House, there is the spirit of a woman, or at least, part of her. The woman wears a brown dress and walks the house in the dead of night. There are no other descriptions as to her appearance, due to the simple fact that she has no head. No one has yet to suggest that the decapitated figure has any connection to the man with the ax, but it's an interesting coincidence!

There is at least one other report of a Huguenot haunting at the Jean Hasbrouck House (yes, there were a lot of Hasbroucks in the area). Unlike the other anonymous ghosts on the street, this one has been identified as the spirit of Elizabeth Hasbrouck, who lived in the house until her death in 1928. Some people have claimed to have made direct contact with her ghost during a séance conducted there.

There may even be more spirits wandering along the old street. As the area has had more than its share of history, it has all the necessary ingredients for hauntings. Take a stroll along Huguenot Street some day, and imagine what life must have been like there hundreds of years ago, the tragedies and hardships the street has seen. Think hard about what the people were like, and if you are lucky, you might actually glimpse one of them.

The Abraham Hasbrouck House built in 1712.

"THEIR TIME"

It seems that for every lecture or book signing I do, I receive at least a half a dozen leads on other potential hauntings. This story is the result of one such event where a woman briefly informed me about the strange occurrences in a home/office in Middletown, New York. Several months later, I received a letter from her inviting me to come to investigate and hear the full story. While I never quite know what to expect on these visits, this was clearly one case of where I got more than I bargained for.

It was a clear, cold winter's day, made all the more bleak by a neighborhood that had definitely seen better days. The large Victorian home was on one of the main roads in Middletown, and Saturday shoppers buzzed up and down the street taking no notice of the house. Nor should they have, as it looks just like any other house on the street. Even if you were to drive by late at night and see figures moving about the lighted rooms, casting shadows upon the windows, you would think nothing of it. Unless, of course, you were aware of the fact that no living soul was inside that house at the time.

I was again accompanied by Bob Strong, and we were greeted at the door by Beth, the woman who had originally contacted me. As we entered, we were immediately struck by the wonderful woodwork. It had obviously taken quite a lot of effort restoring the place and the fine result was another reminder that they just don't build homes like that anymore. Perhaps that is why the unseen inhabitants are so reluctant to leave.

We placed our coats and equipment in the kitchen and were informed that the owner would soon be there. Other people began to arrive and I silently wondered just how many eyewitnesses were involved. Many places I investigate involve a single eyewitness who rather quietly relates his tale. This investigation was quickly taking on the atmosphere of a party, not that we objected to the hors d'oeuvres that were being set before us.

Once everyone had arrived, the dozen or so of us moved into the parlor. Not being sure where to begin, I decided to get some background on the owner and the others present. Most of those present were related and were using the house for offices. The adults were all educated professionals, each seeing varied groups of clients and patients in the course of their businesses. It was clear that there was no way any of them would benefit by fabricating stories—ghosts are not generally conducive to better business practices.

The first to relate her story was a thirteen-year-old girl who had been staying in one of the upstairs rooms a year earlier. Walking into the hall, she had been confronted by a woman in a black lace dress and tall high heels.

The woman also wore a hat with a veil, which did not fully hide her pasty white face and brilliant red lips. The frightened girl knew that this was not a living woman. In fact, she had the distinct impression that this specter was appearing to her exactly as its mortal body had appeared in its coffin. The deathly figure started to float toward the girl, and she ran back into her room and slammed the door. Fortunately, nothing followed her.

Several others had also caught a glimpse of this woman in black, all of them noting in particular the contrast of the bright red lips against the unnaturally white face. A different woman in black had also been seen on at least one other occasion. The owner's mother was seriously ill and was being cared for by one of her daughters in an upstairs bedroom. The daughter left the room for just a few minutes, and when she returned, the mother said, "What a nice woman that was who came in to talk to me!"

The mother went on to clearly describe this woman who wore a plain black dress that was somewhat Amish in its appearance. The woman in black said she had not been in Middletown for many years and wanted to know how the town had changed during that time. It seemed as if she was not familiar with anything that had occurred for many decades. It also seemed as if this woman in black had no problem entering a locked house that only contained two living people, and then leaving again without being seen or heard.

Stories then came out about a third woman seen in the house. This one was shorter and stockier than the figure with the bright red lips. She looked to be in her 60s and wore a beige blouse. One day, one of the occupants left her office on the second floor and saw this figure hovering over the staircase. The woman stopped and stared at the apparition in amazement. The ghostly figure in the beige blouse suddenly looked back at the woman, and seemed stunned that she was visible! Obviously upset at being seen, the figure in beige "ran" down the stairs. Curiosity overcoming fear, the woman ran after the figure which simply disappeared *through* the cellar door without a trace.

It is not only the spirits of women that haunt this house, however. A man's heavy footsteps are often heard on the second floor as well as on the staircase. On many occasions, when *no one* was on the second floor, the sounds of a couple dancing could clearly be heard, the man in hard-soled shoes, the woman in high heels. This second floor and staircase seem to have the most activity, especially between the hours of 10 pm and 7 am. It has gotten to the point where everyone in the house refers to those hours of strange events as "their time," referring to the ghosts who seem to want their privacy.

One of the women who works in the house had forgotten her coat late one night and when she went back upstairs to her office to retrieve it, she had a frightening encounter that she did not care to discuss in detail. Suffice to say she now refuses to return upstairs regardless of what she has forgotten—if it is during "their time." Similarly, if anyone ever needs to come into the house early in the morning, they knock, open the door and announce their presence, lest they surprise the spirits who jealously guard their time alone.

Even if one was to suspect that these phenomena were the result of some kind of mass hysteria or the power of suggestion, many clients and patients who know nothing of the house's unnatural inhabitants have reported hearing footsteps and doors slamming, where no one was visible. Several people have remarked that they have driven by late at night and have seen lights on in a back office on the first floor, with people moving around inside. They assumed it was the owners or employees working late. They assumed wrong. No one was in the house on those occasions.

There are numerous stories about the large cat that lives there, a cat who stares intently at thin air, or suddenly runs as if something is coming toward him. Witnesses have seen objects move, such as the ashtray on the coffee table that slid across the table several times right before their eyes. Two chairs in the kitchen are always found lined up side by side facing the dining room, even though the previous night they were placed around the table. Water faucets constantly turn themselves on full force, even though plumbers have given assurances that nothing is broken. There is the tapping of a cane, a wrapping on the door and the occasional loud crash, all without apparent cause.

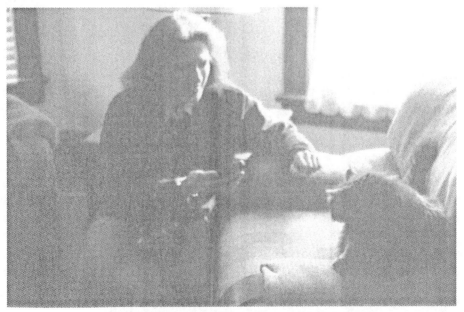

The cat is not pleased as I get some high EMF
readings by the chair on which he is sitting.

A closet door in a second floor office refuses to remain closed, and can often be heard slamming when no one is near it. An afghan disappeared from another office and throughout the day a deathly chill filled the air. Suddenly the afghan reappeared in its proper place, and the chill immediately left the room. Kitchen cabinets open and close by themselves. Doors and windows lock by themselves. Beds shake violently. A computer that had been turned off, printed out a page of mysterious writing one night. A bed creaked as an indentation was made in the covers as if someone was sitting down, but no one could be seen. In short, dozens of different bizarre and inexplicable occurrences have been witnessed by dozens of people over the span of many years.

Is there any kind of evidence to back up the reports of these apparitions and events? In this case, there actually are some compelling facts to strengthen the case for hauntings. A neighbor, who has lived nearby for many decades, was innocently asked about the previous owners. She explained that at the turn of the century, two sisters married two brothers and built identical houses in Middletown. When one of the husbands died, his widow moved into her sister and brother-in-law's house (the house in this story), where the three of them lived the rest of their lives. One sister was tall and thin and used to like wearing high heels and bright red lipstick. The other sister was short, stocky and often wore her favorite beige blouse.

It is a natural reaction upon hearing a story like this to ask, "Why do you stay here?" This question was posed, and some of the answers only added to the mystery of the place. The general feeling is that although often unnerving, the ghosts do not make the living feel threatened in any way. On the contrary, in many instances they have been very protective.

In the years after the sisters and the one husband died, the house was used for many things, including a daycare center. (That didn't last because the children were always very agitated in the house. I wonder why.) The house was then left unoccupied for several years. In an area where a house abandoned for just several days is a prime target for broken windows and vandalism, this house somehow remained untouched.

One cold day one of the women entered the house to find it was over 90 degrees inside. Knowing that the thermostat was always kept low, she ran into the kitchen to find flames shooting out of the stove. A gas line in the stove had ruptured, and the resulting inferno had been hot enough to melt the enamel on the sides of the stove. However, even though there had been intense heat generated by tall flames that had been burning for hours, nothing else in the kitchen had so much as been singed. The stove had been against a wall just an inch from a window with curtains, and neither the woodwork nor the fabric showed the slightest signs of damage.

On another occasion, a snowfall had covered the steep back stairs. One woman was in the process of brushing them off when she slipped and lost her balance. She struggled to remain standing, knowing that hard steps and an even harder pavement awaited her.

"Then there was that terrible, sickening moment that I knew I was going to fall backwards. I was so far over that there was nothing on earth that could stop me," she explained. "I closed my eyes and braced for impact, but there was nothing. I was suddenly standing perfectly straight on the stairs! It was as if someone, or something, had caught me and stood me safely back up."

With protection like that, it's easy to see why they are not too eager to rid the house of its original inhabitants.

After jotting down several pages of notes regarding these numerous events, we decided to look around and take pictures. I had also brought along the EMF meter. Switching it on, I found that the parlor in which we had been sitting had somewhat higher than normal readings. The staircases and a few of the offices were normal and nothing felt out of the ordinary. However, as Bob and I stood in the center of the room in which the afghan had disappeared, a deathly chill passed through us going from right to left. The temperature seemed to drop by at least forty degrees and at that moment the EMF meter spiked to its highest reading. The icy air persisted for 10 to 15 seconds, and the moment it passed, the meter returned to zero.

(One of the advantages of using a scientific instrument is that it is unaffected by the imagination of the user. While the power of suggestion might have caused Bob and I to feel cold, it could not have caused the meter to alter its readings so dramatically.)

All eyes were now on this office, and I placed the meter on the floor, in contact with no one, and several of us stood around in a circle and waited. A few minutes later, another chill swept through (in the same direction—from right to left), and once again the reading on the meter went up, and then back down as the cold disappeared.

The "disappearing" afghan is draped over the chair in the
room where the cold spot and EM field passed through us, twice.

We eagerly explored the rest of the house, and again found unusually high readings near the closet that can be heard slamming. The rest of the house appeared "clean." It should be mentioned that the cat was clearly upset by all the activity, and whether it was from all the humans present, or something inhuman, he retreated to the basement and could not be persuaded to return.

Several months after this visit, I received another call from Beth with an update. There had been an incident where a strange knocking sound (not heard by everyone in the house) had alerted them to the presence of an unsavory and potentially dangerous character on their porch. The police were called, the man ran away, and no one was harmed. They believe it was the ghosts who had alerted them to this intruder.

The people who work in the house have also been doing some detective work, and have not only discovered more history about the original owners, but have discovered their grave sites, as well. Since these new discoveries, the ghosts have been very quiet, which one would think would be a good thing. However, Beth is currently looking for some kind of sign from the old inhabitants, as she and her colleagues are now considering buying the place.

I doubt that Beth has anything to worry about. Considering the fact that these ghosts are among the noisiest, most active apparitions on record, their silence would seem to be a resounding declaration of approval. Perhaps these restless spirits have simply been waiting for responsible, caring owners to watch over their beloved home. And perhaps, with the passing of the years, they will finally reconcile themselves to the fact that "their time" on earth has passed.

WHERE THERE'S SMOKE...

Where there's smoke, there's fire, or so the old saying goes. However, like most old sayings, it isn't always so. Sometimes, where there's smoke, there's a ghost.

Such was the case with a house on West Nyack Road in Rockland County. When the "Martins" moved into their new house, there was a bit of cleaning up to do as the place had been unoccupied for nearly fifteen years. Above the stress of moving and getting things in order, Mrs. Martin felt an inexplicable uneasiness, as if she was always being watched. Every time the feeling became the strongest, the air suddenly filled with the odor of stale, musty tobacco smoke. As no one in the house smoked, the mystery only deepened.

Then one day, the Martin's adolescent daughter came running down the stairs looking frightened and pale. She said there was an old man in a long, black robe upstairs. Upon examining all the rooms, no one was found, but the daughter knew what she had seen with her own two eyes. And nobody could deny what their noses sensed—the heavy aroma of tobacco smoke.

There were to be more sightings of the man in the black robe. Several people saw him in the house, and on one occasion, the Martin's son saw the man walking in the yard. However, as unnerving as the spirit's presence was, the Martins never felt threatened by it, and they tried to deal as best they could with the unusual situation. If only they had answers to the ghostly riddle of the heavy-smoking apparition in the long, black robe...

One day, out of the blue, they got their answers. Two rather elderly ladies showed up on their doorstep, made their apologies for intruding, but requested that they be allowed to look around. In their younger days, they had spent a lot of time at the house. It had belonged to their kind, old uncle, who had been a judge. Since the connection between judges and long, black robes did not escape the Martins, they asked the ladies if their uncle had smoked. The answer was a resounding, "Yes!" In fact, he smoked so incessantly that it was the principle cause of the judge's demise.

It was no doubt a relief to discover the identity of their ghostly resident, as much of a relief discovering that you have the ghost of a dead judge in your house can be, that is. In time the judge's appearances grew less frequent, until they stopped altogether. The stale, smoky odor also eventually disappeared. Perhaps he realized he had been disturbing the family and put an end to his activities. Or, perhaps, the old judge was called on to a higher court.

TREASON AND DEATH

Many ghost hunters and psychics claim that the spirits of the dead cannot harm the living. This is not an opinion I share. At the very least, ghosts elicit fear, and no one should have to endure being afraid in his own home. At worst, the negative energies of an angry, vengeful spirit can have serious consequences on a person's physical, emotional and mental well-being. In the following case, just such a spirit may have actually caused the death of two innocent people in Haverstraw, New York. While the seeds of this tragic event actually may have been planted in the year 1780, the deaths and investigation took place in the 1960s, where this story will begin.

In 1965, an 18th century house overlooking the Hudson River was purchased by two women. One of the women, "Mary," was an editor from New York City. The other woman, "Laura," was recently divorced with a two-year old daughter. Prior to moving into the house, the mother of the little girl was always upbeat. Despite recent disappointments in relationships, Laura was always optimistic about the future and looked forward to raising her child in such a beautiful place.

However, shortly after moving in, her personality began to change. Laura did not seem to be herself and even started to claim that she would never leave that house alive. While Mary was puzzled by such comments and changes in behavior, she had no idea that her friend's words were to come true.

One Sunday, after having been in the house only eight weeks, Laura put her two-year old daughter in the car and left for a drive. That was the last time they were seen alive.

At some point in the following four days, Laura drove to Newburgh, New York. There, she altered the car's exhaust so that the deadly fumes would fill the interior. Then she got back inside the car, closed the windows, and witnessed her only child breathe her last breath, moments before she also expired. On Thursday, the bodies were finally discovered, and just a few days after the funeral, even stranger things began to happen in the old house by the river.

Mary became acutely aware of someone or something trying to get her attention, or more accurately, actually trying to communicate with her. There were the sounds of someone banging on the doors when no one was there. There were footsteps throughout the house when Mary was alone. Then there were the overwhelming feelings of being watched. Yet it was stronger than that, it was a palpable, unnerving presence that drove Mary to begin drinking to try to numb those feelings. Finally, she realized she needed help.

In the 1960s, the man to call about such things was the country's first and foremost ghost hunter, Hans Holzer. Curious, yet wisely skeptical, he visited the house with the psychic medium, Ethel Johnson Meyers. (It must be noted that in order to assure that there were no preconceived notions, Ethel was never told anything about the location or events involved with the cases she was asked to investigate. She knew nothing of the recent suicide or past history of the house and area when she arrived.) As Ethel settled down and entered a trance-like state, Mary and the others present fully expected that they would soon be in contact with the tormented spirit of Laura. As unsettling as that would have been, they were at least braced for the experience. However, no one was prepared to deal with the ghost they actually confronted.

Instead of the remorseful voice of Laura asking forgiveness for taking the lives of her child and herself, a very different voice emanated from the medium. Quickly and suddenly, there were paranoid, fearful words from a young woman who kept insisting she must look out the window to see if *they* were coming. At first, it was difficult to comprehend what the panicked woman was talking about, but gradually her story came to light.

It seems that the spirit said her name was Jenny, and that she worked for someone by the name of Joshua Smith. The year was 1780, the country was at war, and Jenny and Smith being loyal to England, had helped three men escape from the Americans. When Jenny's part in the escape became known, she was beaten and strangled to death in that house.

So, it actually was not the recently departed spirit of Laura that roamed the halls and banged on doors, as everyone expected. It was, in fact, the tormented soul of the murdered Loyalist that haunted that house, seeking retribution for her suffering.

The angry and confused spirit of Jenny soon became too much for the medium to handle, and she was forced to break off communication. With calm restored, the medium went on to describe how this vengeful spirit had *taken over* Laura soon after she moved in. Laura's change in personality was a result of this possession, and ultimately it was what drove her to commit suicide. Once Laura was gone, the spirit had turned her attentions to Mary, who had fortunately sought help before it was too late. Steps were then taken to send Jenny's spirit where it belonged, but even if those efforts were successful, two innocent lives had already been taken.

The task then remained to find out if there was any truth to the story Jenny had told through the medium. It was soon discovered that Joshua Smith was not only the name of a man who had lived nearby, but that he was a Loyalist and he had helped three men escape—some rather famous men, in fact.

During the Revolutionary War, General Benedict Arnold betrayed the Americans and passed vital information about the fort at West Point to the British officer, Major John André. That meeting had taken place at the home of Joshua Smith in Haverstraw. It was from that point that three men, Arnold, André and a servant, began their attempt to escape. While Arnold succeeded and eventually went to England, André was captured, tried and eventually executed in Tappan, NY.

Again, it must be clear that Ethel Johnson Meyers had no previous knowledge of the current events in the house, and certainly no idea of what had transpired almost two hundred years earlier. Yet even with the startling information she received, there are some questions to be answered.

For instance, there is no historical record of Jenny or of a murder of a young woman in the manner she described. However, servants were seldom considered important enough to write about, and traitors were often treated very harshly by local patriots.

Also, the actual Smith house in which the conspirators met was demolished in 1929 (there is a Treason House historic marker on the grounds of Helen Hayes Hospital to show the site). The house in which the two women lived in the 1960s could not have been the house involved in the initial meeting. However, while this was not *the* Joshua Smith house, this house was on the river by the ferry that was used to go across to Westchester. It is possible that the conspirators waited for the ferry in Jenny's house, and had ordered her to keep a sharp lookout until they had made their escape. If Jenny's role in the struggling nation's greatest act of treason had become known, a violent death would not have been an unexpected fate for the guilty servant.

Although there are still many questions about this case, there are far more compelling answers. An argument of coincidence or prior knowledge cannot be supported. So, if the facts of these events are as they appear, this Haverstraw haunting is one of the most dangerous and terrifying cases on record. If true, the angry spirit of a woman murdered two hundred years earlier was directly responsible for driving another woman to commit murder and suicide.

One question does still remain. Were they successful in removing Jenny's spirit from the house thirty years ago? Or, did they simply manage to temporarily appease the angry ghost? Betrayal, anger and violence leave deep scars, and we can only hope that the old house in Haverstraw has been healed for good.

A turn of the century photo of the Joshua Smith "Treason House."
People have claimed to see the ghosts of Benedict Arnold and Major André
throughout the Hudson Valley for hundreds of years.
Photo courtesy of John Scott.

THE HAUNTED BARN

A recent study showed that older homes and buildings across America are disappearing at an alarming rate as they are being leveled to make way for larger, modern structures. Rockland County has seen a good portion of this trend as developers and owners often find that starting from scratch is easier and more lucrative than restoration. One type of house that is fading from the Rockland landscape is the old Dutch Colonial. It is a shame to lose such wonderful pieces of architecture and history, and as a high percentage of these old homes appear to be haunted, we may be losing a rather unique type of history.

One Dutch Colonial that is no longer with us was known as the Murphy-Campbell house on Western Highway near the old bridge that crossed the Hackensack Creek. Actually, the house itself does not seem to have been the site of any unusual activities. However, the barn had more than enough frightening spiritual energy to make up for whatever the house lacked.

The earliest incidents involved one of the house's occupants who decided to go out to the barn to play her guitar. Absorbed in her playing and singing, she suddenly realized that hers was not the only voice accompanying her guitar. There was another woman's voice, and it was definitely coming from somewhere in the barn. No doubt expecting that someone was playing a prank, she thoroughly searched the entire barn, and found no one. Completely unnerved, her musical interlude came to an abrupt halt.

On another occasion, one of the children and his dog were playing in the barn. Suddenly someone, or something, appeared hanging in the air above them and in a heartbeat they turned and ran out. They had been so terrified by the apparition that from that day both the child and the dog refused to ever step foot back into the barn.

As is typical in such cases, fear is often accompanied by curiosity. As afraid as someone might be, it is only human to want to know why a haunting is taking place, especially one filled with the frightful and sad feelings witnesses described.

The family finally got some answers when they learned that many years earlier, a young woman had hung herself from the rafters of the barn. Had she realized, too late, what a terrible mistake her suicide had been, and was she now trying to sing and play among the living once again? We may never know, as the house and barn are now gone.

However, that is not always the end of the story. Occasionally, new homes going up over the site of a tragedy "inherit" the energies trapped there. Remember as you hunt for a new home, that just because no one ever lived there before, it doesn't mean that no one ever died there.

LOST HIS HEAD

The most famous ghost story in America is undoubtedly *The Legend of Sleepy Hollow,* by Washington Irving. What child has not heard the fearful tale of Ichabod Crane and the headless horseman? In addition to Sleepy Hollow's best-known headless resident, Irving made other Hudson Valley legends famous, as in his story *Rip Van Winkle.* Irving's works not only helped to put the Hudson Valley area on the map, he helped bring America into the international world of literature.

After having lived in Europe for many years, as well as having traveled throughout the prairie lands of America, Irving made his home at Sunnyside in Tarrytown. Some people claim that to this day, he still resides in his beautiful mansion. There are reports that Irving's spirit walks the halls and rooms of Sunnyside, and that he particularly favors the tower known as the Pagoda. It seems to be poetic justice that the man most known for his ghost story would pass on and create one of his own.

Washington Irving may still walk the halls of Sunnyside.

Thinking that the Irving haunting story would be a great addition to the ghost stories of the Hudson Valley, I contacted Sunnyside for details. After no one returned my calls for several weeks, I kept trying. Finally, I was actually able to speak to someone, although it was of no use. I was curtly informed that it was "company policy" to not discuss such things.

Anyone can certainly appreciate that those in charge desire to maintain the site with the greatest of historical accuracy and integrity, but something is amiss here. Doesn't it seem rather ironic that in the home of the author of the country's most popular ghost story, ghost stories are off limits? Wouldn't this have been exactly the type of story Irving himself would have written about? Perhaps that is why the spirit of Washington Irving still roams around Sunnyside, trying to correct this case of poetic injustice. Whoever arrived at this policy must have lost his head.

***

While I was taping a segment for a Travel Channel show on haunted places in Sleepy Hollow, New York during the Spring of 2001, the director told me that the staff at Sunnyside had been cooperative and ghosts were no longer a forbidden subject in Irving's house.

If you do visit Sunnyside, be sure to ask if the owner is at home.

THE SPIRITS OF BANNERMAN'S ISLAND

In Dutchess County there is a rocky little island in the Hudson River—an island whose size belies its wealth of history. Though not quite seven acres, this piece of land contains hundreds of years of lore and legend, as well as a literally explosive recent past. While its official name is Pollopel Island, it is popularly known as Bannerman's Island, thanks to the entrepreneur who built a castle upon it early in the 20th century. Castles are always prime haunting territory, but this island was considered haunted long before a single stone was set in place.

Bannerman's Island and castle.

By the time the Dutch arrived in the Hudson Valley in the 1600s, Pollopel Island already had a long-standing reputation. The Indians in the area believed it to be haunted, and even those brave enough to venture to the island in daylight would never set foot on it at night. This made it an ideal place for the Dutch to seek refuge whenever the prospect of hostilities with the Indians arose. Yet even though at first they looked to the island as a place of safety, they too, came to regard it as being haunted.

In addition to a belief in evil spirits, the Dutch believed there were also evil goblins who were led by the worst goblin of all, the Heer of Dunderberg. These goblins were supposed to be responsible for causing storms and strong winds that made river navigation treacherous. As if this wasn't enough to scare sailors on their first journey upriver, the Dutch used to get these new sailors drunk and leave the poor terrified men on the island while they completed their business to the north. On the way back, they would pick up the sailors who had hopefully conquered their fears during their brief stay on the island.

Early in the 18th Century, a ship called the *Flying Dutchman* was carrying passengers up the river to Fishkill. Whether caused by the angry Heer of Dunderberg, or simply by the volatile valley weather, a terrible storm arose as the ship approached Pollopel Island. The captain of the ship tried his best to save his vessel and all the lives aboard, but the storm overwhelmed the *Flying Dutchman*. The ship sank just to the south of Pollopel, resulting in a terrible loss of life.

From the time of that tragedy, generations of fisherman and sailors claimed to hear strange things in the waters around the island. During storms, they believed they could hear the phantom captain of the *Flying Dutchman* still shouting his desperate commands to the long-dead crew. The presence of this local ghost ship must have gone far to enhance the aura of mystery and fear about the island.

During the Revolutionary War, the British were of far greater concern to the locals than spirits. The waters near Pollopel were obstructed by chains and spiked posts in an attempt to prevent British warships from gaining control of the river. George Washington issued orders calling for buildings to be constructed on the island to house munitions and prisoners, although it is not certain if these projects were ever completed. In the more tranquil post-war years, the island became a spot for recreation and a kind of outpost for fishermen.

Over a hundred years later, Pollopel Island would return to military purposes, although in a rather unique way. The Scottish immigrant Francis Bannerman bought the island in 1900 to house his vast amounts of firearms, ammunition and equipment. By buying huge quantities of army surplus, Bannerman had made himself the foremost dealer of these military goods, selling both by catalog and from his store in New York City. Not only did Pollopel provide the perfect location to store his inventory (New York officials were not keen on the idea of Bannerman's enormous amounts of gun powder being stored in the heart of the city), it gave Bannerman the opportunity of using his growing wealth to build his dream home, or dream castle, as the case may be.

Based upon authentic Scottish castles, Bannerman himself designed the huge stone home, as well as the storehouses and other buildings. To facilitate the construction of docks and breakwaters, Bannerman bought aging ships and had them sunk along the shore and covered with concrete. One tugboat captain who had been very fond of his vessel had asked Bannerman if he would please tell the workmen that before they sank it, they make sure that he was far enough down river so that he didn't have to witness his beloved ship's demise. Either the request was not forwarded to the workmen, or they didn't take it seriously, because just as the captain was departing the island, the tugboat was sunk before his eyes.

The captain, infuriated by what he considered to be a personal affront, shook his fist and hurled curses at Bannerman. He swore that he would return, that Bannerman had not heard the last of this old captain. While it's doubtful that anyone at the time took him seriously, there is a chance that the angry captain's threats turned out to be more than just mere words.

A lodge was built on the site of the sunken ship and in its basement was a workshop. For years, employees down in the workshop claimed to hear the ringing of a ship's bell beneath them, where the old tugboat bell would have been. It was the distinct double ringing that a ship used to signal that it was going in reverse. The belief soon arose that the spirit of the angry captain had returned and that he was trying to reverse his ship and get it away from the island.

Notwithstanding the ghostly captain's efforts, the tugboat remained, construction continued and the storehouses were completed and filled. Francis Bannerman died in 1918, but his family continued the lucrative business. However, not all was to be peace and quiet on Bannerman's Island. There were several accidents over the years, accidents which are to be expected handling vast amounts of live ammunition and powder. However, in 1920 there was one unexpected explosion of massive proportions. The blast was so powerful that it propelled a stone wall over a thousand feet across the river and onto the eastern shore, creating a large obstruction on the train tracks. Windows were shattered for miles around. Pieces of buildings, as well as pieces of the island itself, were hurled into the water.

Despite the terrible destruction, the business survived and continued on for another fifty years. However, the family decided to move its storehouses to a more convenient location on Long Island. The Bannermans continued ownership of the castle and island until 1968, when the entire property was sold to the state of New York. There were plans for restoring the castle and turning the island into a park, but the real death blow came the following year. A fire broke out, decimating the castle and other buildings. It appeared as if the haunted island had once again reclaimed its abode for the dead.

In the years before this disaster, however, caretakers and their families lived happily on the island. Yet on many occasions, strange things occurred to remind the occupants of the mysterious reputation of the place. Many times late at night, the sound of a horse running across the drawbridge could plainly be heard. There was only one small problem with this; there were no horses on Bannerman's Island!

There was also a strange whistling sound that could be heard moving around the island. It was an odd, high-pitched whistling sound for which no one could ever find a source. This, combined with the ringing bell, ghost captain and phantom horse helped to insure that the ancient Indian beliefs that the island was haunted would be perpetuated for generations to come.

Today, Bannerman's Island is indeed a dangerous place, although not due to the spirits. The remaining stone walls could collapse at any time, and pathways have deteriorated and are filled with debris (not to mention the snakes, biting insects and poison ivy). Deceptively strong currents around the island should also discourage curiosity seekers. However, there may be hope for the future of Bannerman's Island. Efforts are underway by The Bannerman Castle Trust to raise money to stabilize the structures and restore the walkways so that visitors can once again return.

While it would be wonderful to see this group quickly succeed, there is an alluring air of mystery about the ruins of a castle on a desolate, rocky island in the river. Such a setting would be perfect for a Hollywood ghost story. However, regardless of the island's future, it will always be known as the perfect setting for a Haunted Hudson Valley ghost story.

NOTE: Contributions and inquiries to The Bannerman Castle Trust can be directed to: P.O. Box 843, Glenham, NY 12527, or (845)-831-6346. And thanks to the Trust's president, Neil Caplan, for supplying information for this story.

CAT IN THE KITCHEN

Regardless of how large a house is, people attending a party always seem to congregate in the kitchen. The kitchen is usually a room of warmth and happiness. Unless, of course, that kitchen is haunted.

A house on a corner of Broadway near the downtown area of Nyack seems to have just that problem. Soon after moving in, the new owners noticed their cat was engaging in some rather odd behavior. The cat was always reluctant to enter the kitchen, and when it did, rather than going straight across the floor it always seemed to walk "around" something. It was as if there was an object or person in the middle of the floor that the cat was trying to avoid.

Then there were the noises—strange noises coming from the kitchen at all hours of the night. At first, the sounds were attributed to the cat, but that excuse was quickly dismissed when it was clear that the cat was nowhere near the kitchen at those times. The owners began looking for any rational explanations, even as disturbing, indescribable sounds continued and intensified. Rather than being a gathering place of warmth, the kitchen of their new home was becoming a place of fear and uneasiness.

Not wanting to attract attention or ridicule, the owners nonchalantly began asking neighbors what they knew about the history of the house. At first, nothing of interest came to light. Then, finally, an older neighbor quietly admitted that something terrible had once occurred in the house. A former owner had died there. In fact, she had committed suicide in the kitchen.

Was the spot on the kitchen floor that the cat always avoided the actual spot where the woman had taken her own life? Does some type of residue or energy remain locked there, something that the animal instinctively senses? Do the noises signal the woman's attempt to let the world know she is still in torment, and has found no relief from her suicide?

In any event, it is just one more example of the importance of dealing with your own problems before they become someone else's.

THE PIG GHOST AND THE OTHER HEADLESS HORSEMAN

Animal ghosts are more common than one might think. From beloved cats and dogs who still faithfully search for their masters, to horses who continue to gallop through another world, both ancient legends and modern day hauntings around the world are filled with animal spirits. The Hudson Valley may be unique in one respect, however, as it may possess the one and only ghostly pig—an evil ghostly pig, at that.

The area this pig was said to haunt was a stretch of the old Albany Post Road leading to the town of Fishkill, New York. In fact, this area seemed to possess so many frightening apparitions, both human and animal, that it came to be known as Spook Hollow or Hell Hollow. The main concentration of activity on the road took place at Dry Brook, where a short bridge crossed a perilously deep ravine. For over one hundred years, travelers were so terrorized by these menacing spirits that they would either refuse to travel along that road at night, or would avoid it completely.

Two spirits that were often sighted in Dry Brook appeared to be Revolutionary War soldiers. According to historical accounts, there were two unfortunate deaths that did occur in the area during the Revolution. Apparently, 20 American soldiers deserted from the command of General Israel Putnam, due to a lack of food and pay. One deserter attacked an officer trying to stop him. The officer severely wounded the man with his sword, but the soldier still had enough strength to shoot the officer. Both soon died and were buried in a nearby cemetery. Perhaps the nature of their violent deaths caused them to continue to replay the scene in the dead of night along the road. Or perhaps even after death, the soldier continued to search for his freedom and something to eat, while the officer still looked for deserters among those who traveled the road.

A more horrifying specter was that of a headless horseman (not to be confused with the Sleepy Hollow ghost that Washington Irving made famous). This headless horseman did not appear to be restricted by his obvious handicap, as he used to repeatedly chant "jug-o-rum" while grabbing at the terrified stagecoach travelers who urged their horses to run as if their

lives depended upon it (which they just might have). The headless man would attempt to tie his horse to farmers' wagons, or would even jump onto to the wagons, chanting "jug-o-rum" incessantly. There doesn't appear to be any known historical connections that would tie a decapitated, and obviously thirsty, man to that section of road, but it is doubtful anyone ever paused to ask him just what was on his mind.

As frightening as this apparition must have been, the most feared ghost of Spook Hollow seems to have been the pig. It was apparently an enormous hog that would suddenly emerge from the darkness, terrifying the horses and causing them to lose control, racing ahead down the road as fast as they could go. Witnesses claimed that the pig appeared as if he wanted to do some kind of harm to the wagons and their drivers.

The most bizarre account of the demon hog came from a stagecoach driver. The driver said that the creature actually broke itself in half. Then the head and front legs of the hog ran in front of his team of terrified horses, while the rear section ran along by the back of the coach. Just before entering the town of Fishkill, both ends of the ghostly pig reunited. There

was a very loud sound like a clap of thunder, and then the pig simply vanished into thin air.

The ghosts of Spook Hollow continued their fearful nightly routines up until the 1920s. It was in that decade that the old Albany Post Road underwent considerable changes and eventually became the modern, paved Route 9. Whatever alterations the construction crews made to the area, it appeared to break the spell of hauntings. Was there some natural force, perhaps emanating from the deep ravine that had acted like some kind of magnet for spiritual energy, drawing to it the tortured souls of both humans and animals? How did the construction of a new road disrupt this energy?

Even though Spook Hollow now appears to be free of headless horsemen and demon pigs, it wouldn't be advisable to travel this stretch of road late at night carrying a bottle of rum and a pound of bacon.

RINGWOOD MANOR

The most famous haunted house in America may be the Winchester House in San Jose, California. This sprawling, 160-room Victorian mansion was built using the vast fortune made from the sales of the famous Winchester rifles. The heiress to this fortune was Sarah Winchester, and after the deaths of her young child and husband, she came to believe that the tragedies were caused by angry spirits of the untold thousands of victims killed with Winchester guns. Driven by guilt and fear, she sought to shield herself from these vengeful ghosts. On the advice of a psychic, she believed the solution was to build a home that would confuse the ghosts—*a home that she must never stop building.*

Night and day for 38 years (from the years 1884 to Sarah's death in 1922), construction never ceased. In addition to the 10,000 windows, 47 fireplaces and 40 bedrooms, there are countless bizarre features. Among the 467 doors are many that open to blank walls. Several of the 40 staircases lead to nowhere. Decorative and structural items such as posts are built upside-down. All of these peculiarities had but one purpose, to confuse angry spirits who would become lost and unable to get to Sarah Winchester. While the entire idea may seem ludicrous, it is no laughing matter to the hundreds of employees and visitors who have witnessed ghostly figures and heard inexplicable sounds throughout the mansion. In her attempts to thwart the spirits, Sarah Winchester may have inadvertently created a place that actually attracts them.

While the Winchester Mystery House (as it is known today) is clearly unique, the Hudson Valley area has its own mansion built upon the fortunes of war, or at least, the weaponry used to wage it. Ringwood Manor in Ringwood, New Jersey is a spectacular 51-room, 19th century mansion that was made possible by the huge profits realized from the local iron mines. Much of this iron was used to make firearms and artillery pieces for several of America's wars, dating back to before the Revolution. Like the Winchester House, Ringwood Manor owes its existence to the violent behavior of mankind. Also, like the Winchester House, Ringwood Manor appears to be quite haunted.

Ringwood Manor

While I had heard of Ringwood State Park, the possibility of ghosts in the Manor was first brought to my attention in December of 1998. I received a call from a woman who had just taken a tour of the estate with her friend. Both women had felt uncomfortable immediately upon entering the house. There was the distinct sense that something did not want them there. As the tour progressed, the woman's friend began feeling physically ill and they actually had to leave before the tour was completed.

Shortly after, they stopped at a convenience store to get something to drink. The woman's friend started to get out of the car and collapsed. While it was less than a week before she physically recovered from the swift, sudden and mysterious illness, the woman's personality had undergone a change from that day. Her happy demeanor was gone, and she was now prone to dark moods. While such reactions could be attributed to any number of medical conditions, the woman I spoke to believed that some evil presence at the Manor had been the cause of her friend's physical and emotional problems.

Naturally, I was intrigued by the woman's story and decided to do some investigating. However, it was not without some trepidation that I drove up the Manor's long, curved driveway one chilling day in December. (Contrary to the opinion of my friends, I don't actually look for trouble!) I entered the State Park's office and a female employee asked if I needed assistance. I started to explain that I had written the book *Ghosts of Rockland* and was in the process of gathering stories for a new book, when the woman's smile disappeared. Her eyes dropped to the floor, and with vigorous arm movements she began repeating, "No, no, no, no!" I was somewhat taken aback by the strong reaction. While it is not unusual to encounter good-natured skepticism while making such inquiries, I had never before witnessed such vehement denial, especially when I had yet to ask any questions!

As she continued her one-word denials while waving her arms, I tried to get a little clarification as to why she was saying "no." I asked if what she was trying to say was that she personally had no knowledge of any hauntings, or if she did, was it simply a matter of her not believing in ghosts. The answers continued to be "no, no, no." Just a little frustrated, I finally asked if it was against State Park policy to discuss ghosts. Finally, the expressive gestures stopped, she briefly returned eye contact and I received a subdued but positive response. With that she returned to the back office, slammed the door and I got the distinct impression that the conversation was over.

Rather than being disappointed by the exchange, or lack thereof, I was all the more determined and encouraged to pursue the investigation. It was one of the clearest cases of "Methinks the lady doth protest too much" that I had ever seen. I started doing some research and within a few weeks came across a rather lengthy and detailed story of not one, but several Ringwood Manor hauntings!

In the summer of 1965, due to the efforts of local historian Claire Tholl, a nighttime investigation of Ringwood Manor was arranged with ghost hunter Hans Holzer and the psychic medium Ethel Meyers. Tholl had felt a presence in the house on several occasions, and the superintendent had heard footsteps when no one was there. There had been numerous other reports of strange occurrences such as doors opening by themselves and the figure of a man walking the grounds with a lantern.

On one dark night, the superintendent's son was working on a project in the basement of the Manor when he began hearing footsteps on the floor above him. At first he believed it was simply his brother playing a joke, but the joke began to wear thin as the footsteps went on and on. Going upstairs to confront the prankster, he saw that the room above the basement was, in fact, totally empty. Running back to his own house, he found his brother there and discovered that he had not been out that night. There had been, then, no other living soul in the house during the prolonged series of footsteps.

Many others spoke of feeling at least one presence in the numerous rooms and corridors of Ringwood Manor. One man who had worked on the interior restoration also felt a presence, one that he described as clearly being hostile. (This was the same feeling the two women visitors were to experience over thirty years later.) Was this hostility the result of the angry spirits of those killed by weapons from the family's iron, or was there a more local explanation? These questions fell upon the medium, who as always, had been told nothing of the history of the house or region.

Immediately upon entering the Manor, Ethel felt the presence of a man, and "heard" the name Jackson White. Assuming it was the spirit's name, she asked if anyone was familiar with him. Claire Tholl explained that it was not a man's name, but actually the term (now considered to be very politically incorrect) for the interracial group of people who lived in the Ramapo Mountain area. It was likely that some of them had been part of the large staff of servants required to run such a vast estate.

Somewhat surprised by the information already received, the group of investigators proceeded upstairs and sat around a table in a small room that used to be a servant's bedroom. Ethel entered her trance-like state and began to unravel some of the mysteries of the haunted Manor. The primary disturbances appeared to involve two servants, Jeremiah and Lucy, and a former owner of the house. The servants were very agitated, especially Lucy who claimed to be falsely accused of stealing something very valuable. She may have been beaten or inadvertently killed as a result, and still carried the pain and anger of the injustice. Jeremiah, also implicated in the theft, was more concerned with protecting the household from the group that he considered to be nothing more than intruders. The owner, a woman, took those sentiments even further and was openly hostile toward Ethel and the group. She kept repeating that she wanted them all to leave *her* house.

From other information the medium produced, Claire Tholl thought that the people involved were from the period of the second half of the 19th century. While there was no way to place the servants, the characteristics of the owner did seem to fit one of the family members from that era. Of course, none of this can be taken for absolute fact, but it is interesting that the prevailing emotions the medium detected were those of hostility, and that more than one spirit was intent upon driving away unwanted visitors. These were the same feelings experienced by other people over the span of many decades.

After reading this account, it became clear that I had to take the tour and see the inside of Ringwood Manor for myself. Bob Strong and I went on one of the many brutally hot, dry days in the summer of 1999. The heat had kept the number of visitors down to a handful, and those few sat in the shade of the beautiful gardens while awaiting the next tour. On the lawn in the front of the house, it was obvious that the local concern was iron, as huge metal objects dotted the landscape. Of particular interest was the cannon from the U.S.S. *Constitution* and the enormous mortar that had been made for General Grant during the siege of Vicksburg. Inside, as we were to later discover, there is also an amazing collection of firearms that line the walls of the main hall.

One of the mortars from the siege of Vicksburg during the Civil War, and massive iron links of the type used in the chain across the Hudson during the Revolutionary War.

However, upon entering the house, it was immediately evident that fine art, good taste and money were employed in abundance to divert the attention from the simple iron that had made it all possible. Our knowledgeable guide expertly explained the details of both the maze of rooms that composed the house, and the families who had built and occupied it. While carefully listening to the interesting stories, I nonetheless tried to be aware of any discernable feelings of hostility or anything else unusual, but nothing seemed out of the ordinary. However, a glimpse or two down some of the darkened passageways was enough to convince me that it would not be a place I would care to be alone at night.

Having decided that I would make no mention of my true intentions for the visit (I didn't want to have to go through that again!), Bob innocently asked if the place was haunted. Our guide's eyes quickly darted from side to side before she whispered her answer. She had never experienced anything frightening, but admitted that others had, and she endeavored to never be in the house by herself. On many occasions, she said she did feel as if someone was watching her, but as this is a place that definitely fuels the imagination, it's easy to see how anyone might experience that.

Are their several ghosts roaming the twisting halls of Ringwood Manor? Are some of them hostile to the point of trying to drive away the living from *their* home? According to the official opinion of the state of New Jersey, no. According to dozens of eyewitnesses over the past forty years, the state opinion is wrong—dead wrong.

Regardless of which side of the controversy you stand, Ringwood Manor is a place that should be on everyone's list of places to visit. The gardens are magnificent, the house is an historic treasure, and you certainly can't beat the price of admission (which happened to be free the day we visited, but I'm not sure this is always the case). The entire house is lavishly decorated for special occasions such as Christmas, so if you have already visited in the past you may want to return. Even if the spirits of the dead may not always offer a warm welcome at Ringwood Manor, the living, breathing members of the staff are guaranteed to make up for it.

***

In 2000, I received a letter from a reader shedding light on the bizarre reaction of the park employee. According to a local newspaper article, several years earlier two employees were fired because they spoke about the ghosts of the Manor. Obviously, the woman who confronted me did not want to become the third one to lose her job.

Fortunately, the state of New Jersey has lightened up on this policy since this story was first written. It would be nice to think that my story and my lectures might have had something to do with the policy change, but in any event, I have since spoken with the caretaker and he said it's now okay to mention the hauntings to visitors.

Now we just have to find out if the visitors are okay with the ghosts.

Book Three

HELPING HANDS

This fascinating case began with an e-mail message in November 1999. Peter Martin, who had just read *Haunted Hudson Valley*, wrote to me about a man in Pawling, NY, who had experienced some bizarre events in his home. Although the man, Allan McNett, was in his late eighties, Peter was quick to point out that Allan's memory was sharp and clear, and he was not one to make up stories.

At the time, I was very busy on another project, and having recently finished *Haunted Hudson Valley*, I was not planning on any ghost research for a while. However, rather than file this information for a later date, I felt compelled to call right away. I'm glad I did, for not only did the ensuing meeting uncover a most remarkable story, I formed a friendship that is very dear to me.

Allan McNett was born in the state of Washington in the year 1910. After college, his natural artistic abilities helped him secure a job at Boeing where he made meticulously detailed models of their aircraft, including the famed B-17. During World War II, flat feet may have kept him out of combat, but his razor-sharp mind and skill with word puzzles made him a perfect candidate for the cryptography department of the U.S. Army. He was sent to cryptography school in Pawling, NY, and then served in North Africa. When the war was over, Allan did not return to Washington. He went back to Pawling, because while in school there he had met a beautiful young woman named Helen who was to become his wife of almost 50 years.

In January of 1997, Helen passed away after a long illness. It was then that the unusual events began to happen. About 6 o'clock one morning, Allan was about to start his day with his usual cup of coffee. He went into the kitchen and found a pot of water on the stove that had just come to a boil! He had not been in the kitchen yet that morning, and had he left the water on from the night before it would have all boiled away. In addition, Allan never made his coffee in that manner; he always used the microwave.

Allan McNett's kitchen, where unexplainable events occurred.

Wondering if it was possible that he was getting forgetful, Allan poured out the hot water, put the pot in the sink and went about making his coffee in the microwave. He sat in the living room enjoying his coffee and after a while decided he was going to have some oatmeal. Entering the kitchen, he was startled to see the same pot back on the stove, once again filled with water just coming to a boil! It was as if someone or something had anticipated his wishes and was trying to take care of him.

(At this point, I feel it is important to stress that Allan McNett not only is one of the most intelligent men I have ever met, but his memory is clearly of the finest, almost photographic, nature. For example, he is able to recite every word of every poem he has ever written [and he has written scores of magnificent poems]. He has also memorized lengthy works like the *Rubaiyat,* in their entirety. If Allan claims he did not put those pots of water on the stove, I believe him 100 percent.)

Even more curious events began to occur in the kitchen. Specifically, the flour scoop was often found on the countertop, and it would be full of flour. Allan would return the scoop with its flour back to the drawer, leave the kitchen, and a short time later find the scoop back on the counter neatly filled with flour once again.

One day, a woman who lived nearby was visiting Allan. As they stood in the kitchen, he pointed to the empty countertop and the closed flour drawer and explained what had happened. They then went into the living room and after a short time heard a noise in the kitchen. Going to investigate, the woman was stunned to see the flour drawer open and the scoop full of flour sitting on the counter just as Allan had described.

The woman admitted to me that when Allan first told her the story she quietly thought that he was just getting a bit forgetful in his old age. However, when she saw with her own eyes that the flour scoop was sitting on the counter when no human being had been anywhere near it, she quickly became a believer.

I personally examined the mysterious flour drawer. It was mounted under the top cabinets, and it was clearly not capable of falling open by itself. In fact, it has a kind of hook slot in the back so that the drawer needs to be lifted straight up and then

The flour drawer and scoop.

pulled forward to open. Also, if the drawer had somehow managed to slide open on its own and the scoop had somehow gone up and over the sides and fallen out, one would expect that when it hit the counter it would bounce around and any flour inside of it would go flying across the counter and onto the floor. However, every time the scoop was discovered, it sat neatly on the counter in the same spot with hardly a speck of spilled flour.

There have been other witnesses to this bizarre flour scoop event. A neighbor's boy who helps out with Allan's computer, which is set up in the dining area of the kitchen, was working on the computer while talking to Allan, who was doing dishes. The flour drawer was to their backs, and neither of them heard anything unusual, but for some reason they both turned at the same time and saw the flour drawer once again open with the filled scoop sitting on the counter.

This young man has been witness to two other bizarre events. While chatting with Allan one day they heard strange, faint music and finally tracked it down to an old, unused radio that sat on a bottom shelf in the living room. The boy put his ear near the radio and there was no doubt that the music was coming from its speaker. Trying to shut it off, he found that the knob was already clicked into the off position. Trying all the knobs, nothing seemed to change either the volume or the type of music coming from the radio. They finally decided the only thing to do was to unplug it, but when the boy traced the cord he found the dusty plug laying on the floor, nowhere near the socket! Somehow, an old radio that was not even plugged in had found a way to play music.

Another time, a small tape recorder in the living room started making a buzzing sound. The recorder had not been used for many years, and Allan was not only surprised that it had turned itself on, but that the batteries were still good after such a long time. Trying to shut off the sound with the buttons did not work, so he opened up the back panel to remove the batteries. There were none! Once again, and old electronic item with no power

The attic fan (top of picture) can only be turned on by the wall switch on Allan's right. The switch is about 30 feet from the front door.

source was somehow producing sound.

There was one electrical item in the house that was powered and was expected to work, but only when it was turned on by human hands: the attic fan. However, this did not seem to be the case on many days when Allan would arrive home on a hot afternoon. As he opened the front door, he would hear the attic fan starting by itself. Anyone who has such a fan knows that when it is first turned on, it takes a minute to get up to speed and for the vent slats to open to begin drawing air up. Allan was quite specific that as he was opening the door the fan was just kicking in and the vent slats were just starting to open. Had he left the house with the fan on, it would have already been in a fully operational status.

Despite these inexplicable things going on, at no point did Allan feel threatened by this "spook", as he called it. At some times, like with the radio and tape recorder, it just seemed to be wanting to prove that he was not alone. The boiling water and attic fan incidents indicated that someone was just trying to help. The flour scoop seems to be the most personnel event, perhaps showing that the woman who once used it had not really gone away.

These bizarre occurrences continued for over a year. However, when another man (a talented chef who could prepare meals and take care of odd jobs around the house) moved into the spare bedroom, the unusual happenings finally ceased. No more powerless radios played music of the past, no more pots of water began heating themselves.

Had Allan's dear wife Helen returned to let him know he was not alone? Despite being in the other world, had she still tried to take care of the husband she had loved for fifty years? Once someone had moved in with Allan, someone she could trust to help take care of him, had she decided to cease her activities because her husband was now in good hands?

In our initial conversation, Allan remained noncommittal about the "spook" who had kept him company for a year. He said he didn't know what it was, but he also could not say what it was not. However, over subsequent conversations, he has admitted that he feels that maybe it was Helen, after all. Perhaps she had somehow managed to return and drop some not-so-subtle hints that she had never really left him.

Allan and I have become very good friends; we speak several times a week on the phone, and I try to visit him as often as my busy schedule allows. As I sit in his living room and look at the portrait of his beautiful wife, and hear the stories of their happy life together, I feel a comforting warmth. If this is a ghost story, there is nothing cold, dark or sinister about it. It is a wonderful affirmation that true love really does last forever.

Allan McNett passed away on August 8, 2000.

Hopefully, he and Helen are hand-in-hand once again.

A CORPSE IN BED

Strange happenings in the other world were the last thing on the mind of "Jim Ford"; there was more than enough going on in this world to occupy his attention. Jim and his mother had recently returned to their home in Kingston, New York, after an absence of two years, and Jim was looking forward to some well-deserved peace and quiet.

Several years earlier, there was an unpleasant domestic situation with Jim's stepfather. His mother had suffered a nervous breakdown and his stepfather reacted by keeping her isolated and not allowing her any real treatment. Though only in his late teens, Jim had the courage and wisdom to take his mother out of the house and get her professional help. These turbulent years finally looked as if they were coming to an end when his mother recovered, got a divorce and regained possession of the house. It seemed as if Jim and his mother had nothing more to fear. Unfortunately, the real terror had yet to begin.

Jim was now 22, fresh out of college, and working at his new job with an insurance company. He was glad to be back in his old home and had taken a different room than the one he had before he left. His new bedroom was much cooler in the summer and should have allowed him a better night's sleep. However, Jim found sleep in that room almost impossible, tossing and turning and waking many times throughout the night. With his troubles long gone, he should have been able to rest peacefully, but not resting in peace was exactly the problem.

One night, Jim was doing his usual tossing and turning when he flipped over and came face-to-face with the most horrifying apparition one can imagine. He was literally on top of a grayish, glowing figure of an emaciated old woman. Her deep-set eyes, beneath sunken cheeks and wrinkled skin, stared directly into his, just inches away. Jumping back in terror, Jim noticed that she lay motionless on the bed, her arms at her side, looking exactly like a corpse in its coffin.

Jim's self-preservation instinct kicked in, literally. He began kicking and pushing at the figure, sending all his pillows, sheets and blankets onto the floor. The terrifying apparition had no reaction to Jim's frantically flailing arms and legs. Even though everything else had been knocked off the bed, the old lady's glowing corpse remained. Finally, mercifully, it simply vanished into thin air. Except for all of the bedding laying on the floor and Jim's wildly pounding heart, there was no sign that anything out of the ordinary had happened that night.

Jim hesitated to tell his mother, not wanting to upset her, but the horrifying image had so shaken him he had to tell someone. Her reaction was one of polite skepticism, the "yeah, sure, whatever you say" reaction. Of course, it's only natural for someone to be skeptical about such a story and Jim's only proof was the terrifying memory of that face which would forever be burned into his mind.

The next few nights were understandably tense, but fortunately the glowing form of the old lady did not reappear. Yet still, Jim did not sleep well. Then one night he had another visitor, or perhaps the same one, just in a different form. A nearby streetlight always cast a soft, diffuse light through the curtains, but this night something blocked that light. He opened his eyes to see a short, dark figure standing next to his bed. He couldn't make out any features, nor could he even tell whether it was a man or a woman; he only new it was standing right next to him and he felt threatened.

As with the apparition of the corpse in his bed, Jim's immediate reaction was to fight off the intruder. His fists shot out toward the dark, menacing presence, but they struck nothing but air. Also as before, the ghostly figure had no reaction to his attempts to drive it from his room. It simply dissolved, leaving no trace of its presence. The following nights were quiet, although one can imagine they were not very restful. However, the dark figure was to make one more appearance by Jim's bed. Again, fists were useless, and the unwanted visitor disappeared in its own good time.

Thoroughly shaken by these frightening, otherworldly events, Jim sought advice from his mother, who had become very religious since her ordeal with her illness and marital troubles. After carefully listening to all the details of his terrifying story, Jim's mother had two recommendations. First, she told him to hang a cross in his room, which he did. Her other recommendation was for him to throw out the copy of the *Playboy* magazine (the Pamela Anderson issue, to be exact) he kept in his room. Jim admits that despite being desperate for a solution to this haunting, that was one piece of advice he did not follow!

Perhaps the addition of the cross was sufficient, or perhaps the apparitions were content with having made their presence known, but whatever the reason, Jim was not visited by any more spirits in the time he remained in the house. Fortunately, the only visitors he has in his new home are the living, breathing people he invites. While his mother still lives in the house in Kingston, she has never experienced anything out of the ordinary. Still, just to be on the safe side, she did have all of the rooms of the house blessed.

Is there any evidence to corroborate what Jim saw? The house is old enough for several generations to have lived there. The previous owners were a man and his very elderly mother; could she have died in that bedroom, or did she simply desire to return to the place she had known for so many years? It is impossible for us to know for sure, but Jim Ford has all the proof he needs of this ghostly phenomena.

Today, Jim is a successful businessman and is very active in civic affairs. He has a friendly, outgoing manner, and if you were to have any business dealings with him or engaged him in a conversation socially, you would think he would be the last person on Earth to believe in ghosts. But if Jim lets you into his confidence and tells you the story of that terrifying, glowing corpse in bed with him, or of that dark, menacing figure, the truth of his words will make your skin crawl and send a tingle of fear up your spine. And when you close your eyes some night in bed, you might be afraid to open them for fear of coming face-to-face with your own worst nightmare.

A HAIR'S BREADTH

Many homes in South Nyack, NY, have interesting stories to tell. Many were built with the money made by both local industry and distant commerce. Some have the distinctive "widows walks," where wives looked out to the river waiting to see their husbands finally returning home from their long voyages. While the history and architecture of these houses are sufficient reasons to attract our attention, at least one of them attracted attention is very unique way.

"Beth Walker" is a teacher in the South Nyack school system, as well as being a lifetime resident. Her hectic school schedule and busy family life leave little time for flights of fancy, and she would calmly assure anyone who asks that she is "not prone to hallucinations." However, she might also tell you of some experiences from her childhood that might go to show that ghosts can be a part of a normal daily life.

The house in South Nyack in which she grew up is a fine example of 19th century architecture. It was built by a sea captain who raised his family in what was then a very different Rockland County. He was no doubt away from his beloved family for long stretches of time, and it is just possible that his wife and daughters still await his return from a voyage, an eternal voyage from which no one ever returns.

Beth's was a typical American family of the 1950s. They had a comfortable, happy home, but with an odd twist. They were not alone in their home. One of the first signs that they had otherworldly visitors came from the attic. There was an old rocking chair stored up there and periodically they could all clearly hear it rocking back and forth. They would go up into the attic to investigate, but always found that no one was there, there were no windows open to create a breeze, and the chair would be perfectly still. Nothing else stored in the attic could possibly make the distinctive sound of a rocking chair creaking on floorboards. There was simply no rational explanation for the frequent and bizarre sounds. As irrational as it seemed, they felt that it must be a ghost.

The rocking chair was not the only thing in the house that seemed to move on its own. For some reason, thermometers always seemed to disappear. While every household experiences lost or misplaced items, they could always count on their thermometers vanishing. There were also some other items that disappeared, but these would return, and they would return carrying something extra.

Beth and her siblings all had dark brown hair. Her parents both had dark brown hair. The other items that would go missing were the family's hairbrushes. While the brushes would eventually turn up again, they were not returned with dark brown hair in them. On one occasion, Beth specifically searched for her brush on top of a pile of knitting. She distinctly remembered putting both hands on the knitting and pressing down to make sure the brush was not underneath. Leaving the room for just a moment, she returned to find the brush sitting right on top of the knitting she had just so closely examined. 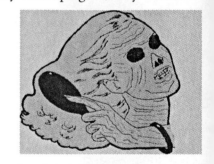 Picking it up, she noticed it was full of strands of red hair. Other family members would have hairbrushes missing for days, only to be returned with strands of blond hair in them.

While the combination of the phantom rocker and the missing thermometers and brushes would be enough for most people to pack up and put their house up for sale, Beth's family learned to live with it. Even though she was just a child, she never felt threatened by any of the strange events. On the contrary, she always felt very secure and comfortable in that house. The only place she was ever afraid was in the basement, but Beth attributes that to the big, scary furnace and ordinary childhood fears.

From the time Beth became aware of the ghostly happenings in the house, to the time she left home for college, spanned about ten years. The disappearing items and self-rocking chair persisted throughout all that time. They may even continue to this day. Just by coincidence, Beth found that one of her students now lives in the same house in which she grew up. When she mentioned the strange happenings she and her family had experienced, the student just gave her an odd look without responding. She wasn't quite sure if the odd look meant that the student was surprised that someone else had experienced the same things, or that the student simply thought she was nuts.

Curiously, the house next door might also have had a restless spirit. It had been owned by a spinster born during the Civil War, who lived there for almost 100 years. After her death, people often claimed to see a woman standing in the window, even though the house was vacant. Ironically, this was the house that came to be known as the haunted house of the neighborhood, not Beth's. Unfortunately, it would now be impossible to find if there was any truth to this haunting as the old woman's beautiful Victorian home was demolished to make way for a parking lot.

It is not often that ghosts leave behind any trace of their appearances, so it would have been fascinating to be able to examine the blond and red hair that continually appeared in the family's brushes. Unfortunately, the phenomena became so commonplace that no one thought to save the phantom strands for analysis. In an age when parapsychology is struggling to boost the supernatural into the realm of provable science, it seems that here was a case where proof was only a hair's-breadth away.

HOUSE OF EVIL

In modern times, the Hudson Valley has become a refuge for families trying to escape the urban problems of New York City, as well as the congestion of Long Island. One family who left the crowded conditions on Long Island and moved north in the 1990s hoped that they would find a better way of life in the rural setting of Warwick in Orange County. Unfortunately, in an attempt to escape the evils of this world, they walked straight into the grasp of evil from the other world.

It had seemed to be the ideal situation. At an auction, "Joe and Marie Cazzerro" purchased the massive 19-room colonial on a quiet, wooded street for what appeared to be a bargain price. Not only did their winning bid include the spacious 18th century dwelling and beautiful grounds, everything in the house from the antique furniture to the clothing to the dishes was thrown into the deal. It was almost as if the previous family had just suddenly gotten up and ran out, leaving everything, but they quickly laughed away that idea. After all, who would ever do such a thing?

Soon after moving in, it became apparent that this had been no bargain. There was an uneasiness throughout the house, a chilling, malevolent presence that affected everyone. There were cold spots, strange footsteps, and objects that would suddenly fly across the room. Family members and visitors complained of feeling disoriented and nervous in the house. There was often a bad odor that could not be traced to any known source.

One of the most terrifying experiences occurred one day when Marie's five-year-old daughter approached her in the backyard. It immediately became evident that the girl was not herself—she had a faraway look and an expression her mother didn't recognize. A mother knows the full range of emotions her child is capable of displaying. The look she now received from her daughter was unlike anything she had ever seen. Apprehension turned to panic when the little girl's lips began to move and she started to speak in an unfamiliar voice. It was no doubt the voice of the very young girl, but Marie also had no doubt that this was not the voice of her daughter.

This strange child's voice began crying for help. The voice insisted that she was at the bottom of the well and needed help. She begged and pleaded for someone to help her out of the well. Terror gripped her daughter's features, yet Marie knew it wasn't really her daughter. The strange voice continued for some time to cry out for help, and then slowly faded away and the tranquil, smiling face of her daughter reappeared. Whatever had come over the girl had passed, and her daughter had no recollection of saying anything about being trapped in the well.

It would be natural to try to dismiss this episode as merely the overactive imagination of a five-year-old. However, even if this had been the case, Marie took some startling photos that may provide some hard evidence to the case for a haunting, and cameras do not have an imagination.

One of the Cazzerro's sons was celebrating his first communion. Marie had taken numerous photos of the event, but had a few shots left over that she wanted to finish so she could bring the film to be developed right away. It was a clear, sunny day, and she knew that the time was between 11:45am and noon. Stepping out onto the deck on the north side of the house (meaning that the sun was high in the sky and to her back) she just took a couple of pictures of the yard. If nothing else, she would have some photos to show her friends back in Long Island how lush and beautiful her property really was.

All of the photos she took that day came out fine, except for the two taken in the backyard. There were unusual patches of light that almost looked like a bright fog. If the film had somehow been damaged, it didn't make sense that only these two would be effected. Taking a closer look, Marie was startled to see that these were not just random spots of light, they appeared to take on definite shapes.

94

One of the fog-like figures looked to be a man in a hooded robe standing just a few yards from the deck. Another spot looked like a man's face—a man with a very menacing expression. As frightening as these misty figures were, the most disturbing feature was actually the barn or large shed that appeared just along the tree line. It's not that the structure doesn't appear solid, it's simply that there was no barn or shed standing in her backyard. Had Marie inadvertently captured a snapshot of the people and buildings from a time a long past? (Due to the some legal concerns that later developed, it was thought best not to release these photos for publication.)

Even though Joe Cazzerro did not spend as much time in the house as his wife and children, he seemed to be particularly vulnerable to all that was going on. His personality changed, he became nervous and agitated, and Marie was worried about his health, both mental and physical. He had never acted this way before moving to the house in Warwick.

The last straw for Joe came late one night. He had been asleep when something startled him awake. Opening his eyes, Joe saw a whitish apparition floating over the bed directly above him. His nerves could stand no more. One family friend put it simply, Joe "flipped out."

Joe Cazzerro left. He left his wife, he left his children, and he left the terrifying house that had made his life miserable and brought him to the brink of insanity. Joe refused to go back to that house, yet Marie insisted on staying, despite all that was happening. This strain on the marriage became too great and divorce was inevitable.

Marie invited her lawyer to the house to discuss the divorce proceedings. The lawyer reported that upon entering the house, she, too, experienced that uneasy feeling. The living room was icy cold. Sitting in the dining room, she felt something brush against her, an unseen figure that passed with such force that it created a breeze. The lawyer's own experiences in the house, coupled with the stories of horror that Marie later divulged to her, brought her to an inescapable conclusion. Marie and the children had to get out of the house. It may not have been the most sound legal advice, but under the circumstances it was the only sane and safe thing to do.

"I told her to get out, just to take the children and get out. I told her to leave everything and get out of there as soon she could," the lawyer said. "But she was very religious and wanted to believe that by burning candles and praying to the Virgin Mary she would be protected from whatever evil was in the house."

The situation eventually deteriorated into a siege—a siege of the dead against the living. Filling her bedroom with religious symbols and burning candles throughout the night, Marie and her children essentially barricaded themselves in her bedroom every night. The children all slept with her, afraid to be in any other part of the house after the sun set.

Desperate for answers, two psychics were invited to come test the "atmosphere." Both immediately felt an evil presence. They also claimed that there were children buried in the basement. (Some old shoes and bits of clothing were later uncovered in the dirt floor, but no bones were found.) After a very short time in the house, they came to the same conclusion as the lawyer: the family should leave as soon as possible.

As the terror continued unabated, Marie finally realized she could not win. She now saw that she had been fighting a losing battle from the day they had moved in, and she did not want her children to become casualties of this bizarre war. Afraid even to take any of the furniture with them, for fear that it would somehow carry along the evil presence, they left the house with nothing. After they were gone, the house looked much as it did when they had bought it—fully furnished, as if the family who had lived there had suddenly gotten up and ran out, leaving everything.

Once out of the house, Marie was anxious to quickly sell it and put the nightmare behind them. Unfortunately, it was not to be, as it was discovered that the water in the area was contaminated. There had apparently been some illegal dumping of toxic waste nearby, and the ensuing contamination made the property unsafe and un-sellable.

One cannot help but wonder whether the chemicals in the water had caused the Cazzerro family to think that they were hearing and seeing things, as well as having a negative impact on their physical health. However, this would not explain the experiences of the people who came to visit, who had not had any of the water or any long-term exposure to possible fumes. And the photos Marie took would also not be affected by the contamination.

It is often said that ghosts cannot harm the living. While none of the Cazzerros was physically injured, I think mental anguish, divorce, and being driven from one's home are harm enough. Many times I have heard people say that they wished that their house was haunted. Hopefully, this story will convince those people to be careful what they wish for. And if after reading this they still don't see reason, I know of an abandoned, fully furnished house in Warwick that's a real bargain.

AN IMAGINARY FRIEND?

The waters of the Hudson River that begin in upstate New York travel a long journey through the highlands, pass through the beautiful valleys and eventually find their way to the sea through a series of islands. One of them is Staten Island, an area rich with history, and therefore a prime spot for hauntings.

The following story, however, does not involve any colonial landmark or famous mansion, just a simple private home on a typical street. The turn-of-the-century, two-family dwellings were close together on this street, allowing on the one hand for a friendly neighborhood feeling, and on the other hand, it allowed the opportunity for everyone to know everyone else's business. When the business of your household involves a ghost, you would be more than likely to try to keep it as quiet as possible.

In fact, a lack of quiet was how this particular haunting began. "Mrs. Joan Angelotti" understood why her husband used to go up into the attic for peace and quiet. In a household with three children (who were home schooled) and a dog, the attic became his little sanctuary where he could take naps, work on the family budget and bills, and just have a few moments to himself.

One afternoon after her husband had gone up to his little retreat, Joan started hearing strange noises right above her head. It sounded like heavy furniture was being moved in the attic. She knew her husband had been very tired and thought he had gone to take a nap. It just didn't make sense that he would suddenly choose to start moving furniture. Climbing the stairs to the attic, Joan opened the door expecting to see her husband panting and sweating from what must have been intense labor by the sounds of it. Instead, she found Mr. Angelotti sound asleep with not a thing in the attic out of place by so much as an inch.

Joan shook him awake and asked what he had been up to. Taking a moment to clear his head, he asked what she was talking about. The two could not come to any agreement as to what had happened—Mr. Angelotti believing the noise must have come from somewhere else, while Mrs. Angelotti stood by her story of the furniture-moving sounds. These heavy scraping sounds were to be heard on several other occasions, sometimes when Mr. Angelotti was up there taking a nap and other times when no one at all was up there.

The family dog also heard sounds and would often stare at a door or hallway and growl protectively. On one occasion, the bathroom door suddenly slammed closed by itself (no windows were open to create a draft) and the dog was very agitated, growling and barking as if an intruder was inside. Joan pulled open the door, not sure what or who to expect, and actually found the unexpected; there was no one to be seen.

While many children have imaginary friends, the young Angelotti children all seemed to share the same imaginary friend. The three of them would hold conversations as if a fourth child was present. They would play hide and seek as if a fourth child was present. They would also play games as four. After a session of coloring and drawing, they would proudly produce

97

four different pieces of artwork.

Imaginary friends are one thing, but Joan felt that her children were carrying this just a bit far. Finally one day, Joan decided to speak to each child separately, and ask about this invisible friend. She had been prepared to explain that it wasn't good to pretend *too* much. She had also been prepared to hear three different descriptions about this imaginary friend, as she assumed each child would have his own idea as to the perfect invisible playmate.

To her surprise and concern, each child innocently described exactly the same thing—a nine-year-old boy in a white polo shirt. To them, he was completely real, and joined in their games and conversations as if he was a living, breathing, child. To make it all the more unnerving, the children looked at their mother as being a little strange for not being able to see the boy who was so plain to their eyes.

While Joan never saw this boy in the white shirt, she did see a small, shadowy figure on numerous occasions. She also experienced those distinct cold spots that often accompany an apparition. As irrational as it seemed, Joan eventually had to come to the conclusion that her home was haunted, and that her children had the ability to see the child as he had been in life. The children continued to include this ghostly boy in their playtime activities for a period of about six years. However, one by one, as they grew older, they seemed to lose the ability to interact with their otherworldly friend.

Naturally curious, Joan asked some older neighbors about the history of the house. Not wanting to sound too strange, she nonetheless tried to get some answers about the unusual and unexpected addition to her family. One couple did recall a young boy who may have fallen ill and died in the house, but they weren't exactly sure as it had happened long ago.

It should be pointed out that during all these years of strange sights and sounds, none of the Angelotti's ever felt afraid. Eventually, all these unusual phenomena subsided and when the children were full-grown they ceased completely. Perhaps one needs the special innocence of childhood to clearly see such apparitions, or perhaps the ghost boy, himself, only wanted to play with younger children.

If you know of a child who claims to have an invisible friend, who sees or hears what you can not, don't be so hasty to dismiss it as youthful imagination. It may not be a case of them seeing something that isn't there. It may just be that you can't see what is right in front of you.

THE RESTLESS SPIRITS OF OAK HILL CEMETERY

> **Help Wanted**: This job will require that you be surrounded by dead people night and day. Two men who previously held this position committed suicide by shooting themselves. Some experience necessary.

Not your idea of the perfect job? You are not alone. Being the caretaker of a cemetery is not everybody's cup of tea. However, for Luke Conroy of Oak Hill Cemetery in Nyack, New York, the position of caretaker has afforded him the opportunity to not only interact with a section of the community that needs his compassionate support, but it has also provided a home for his family.

Compassion appears to be a standard Conroy family trait, with his wife Nancy being a nurse, and in the case of his charming young daughter, who the couple went to Siberia to adopt. In addition, Luke is also a third-year seminary student. Such people are usually not prone to flights of fancy, or bothered by superstition, which makes them excellent choices to live and work on the grounds of a cemetery.

Before moving in eleven years ago, they had not heard of anything unusual happening either in the house or on the cemetery grounds. However, something bizarre occurred the very night they moved in. As anyone who has ever relocated well knows, moving is an extremely stressful and tiring event. For the Conroys, the day was no less exhausting and by evening they were both content to just have all of the boxes inside the house. Unpacking could wait.

Nancy was in the upstairs bathroom getting ready for bed, when she clearly heard the sound of one of the heavy cardboard boxes in the hall outside the bathroom door being dragged across the wooden plank floor. She then heard the bedroom door on the other side of the hall open, the box being dragged in, and the door closing again. She couldn't believe that Luke still had the energy to move anything, let alone one of the heaviest boxes, so she opened the door to ask him what on earth he was doing. No one was in the hall, none of the boxes appeared to be disturbed, and when she went into the bedroom she found Luke tucked in bed fast asleep. Wherever the sounds had come from, it seems that they had actually not come from earth!

She went back across the hall into the bathroom and the moment she closed the door the sounds started again. First was the sound of the heavy box being dragged across the floor, followed by the opening of the bedroom door. This time, she opened the bathroom door right away and the sounds suddenly stopped. The family cat, Bridgett, was sitting in the corner, staring at the bedroom door as if someone was standing there. Nancy went back into the bedroom where Luke was still sound asleep and this time shook him awake.

Explaining what she just heard, she wanted to know if he had been moving any boxes. Still groggy from being awakened, he assured her that he had been doing nothing but sleeping. Exhaustion overcoming any concern, Luke fell right back to sleep. Starting to feel a bit anxious, Nancy entered the bathroom a third time. Once again, the moment she closed the bathroom door there was the sound of the heavy box being scraped across the floor and the door opening and closing. That was all her nerves could take, and she went straight into the bedroom and made Luke get up. The two searched the house from top to bottom, but found nothing.

Fortunately, the strange sounds did not come back the following night, and they settled down to a quiet, peaceful routine. As years passed, an occasional odd event would take place, but nothing that was beyond the realm of possible explanations.

One man, who used to live in the old caretaker's house at the top of the hill, did tell them that as a child he used to play hide and seek among the

The top of Oak Hill Cemetery looking east toward the Hudson River and the Tappan Zee Bridge. Nyack Hospital (on the left in the center of the photo) is directly across the street from the cemetery.

tombstones with some very elusive children who he could never actually catch. There were also stories of individuals seen walking across the cemetery and then seemingly disappearing. Again, none of this could be proven to be anything outside of the normal, although it was nonetheless inexplicable.

Then one day, Luke was in the eastern section of the cemetery trimming grass with a weed whacker. It was a warm May morning with bright sunshine, not the type of day one would consider spooky. As he moved back and forth among the stones, glad to be outside on such a glorious day, he suddenly got the distinct feeling someone was watching him. He stopped for a moment, looked around, saw no one and went back to work. However, the feeling persisted and then grew stronger. Finally, this unnerving, unseen presence grew so overwhelming, Luke admits to actually dropping the weed whacker and *running* away. Later, when he asked the man who grew up in the old caretaker's house about that area, the man matter-of-factly stated that it was a very "active" part of the cemetery.

In contrast to being afraid of something he couldn't see, an event occurred in the spring of 1999 involving something Luke could see, but at first had no reason to fear. The Conroys have two wonderful female black labs (Molly and Daisy), who, true to their breed, are infinitely friendly and playful. Luke takes them for walks on a regular schedule throughout the day. One sunny afternoon, they were returning from their usual route, which brought them south off of Route 9W and across the front lawn heading toward the paved road in the cemetery leading to the house.

After having crossed about half the distance of the lawn, Luke saw a young woman walking down the hill in the south section of the cemetery, in an easterly direction. There was absolutely nothing unusual about her. She looked to be in her twenties, and she was wearing jeans, a jacket that went below her waist, and had glasses and long brown hair that moved in the breeze. Luke expected that when she reached the intersection by the house that she would turn right toward the exit. Instead, she turned left and headed straight toward him.

By this point, Luke had crossed the lawn and was on the paved road perhaps fifty or sixty feet from the young woman. Both Molly and Daisy obviously saw her, too, as they looked straight at her with their tails wagging. Luke stayed on the left-hand side of the road, in case the woman might feel intimidated by two very large dogs, as friendly as they were. He was waiting for the woman to make eye contact with him or at least look at the dogs before he would speak up to reassure her that there wasn't anything to the afraid of.

They drew ever closer, the woman heading north on the road and Luke and the dogs heading south, now only a few yards apart, yet the woman continued to stare intently straight ahead. She never averted her gaze for an instant and made no indication that she even saw Luke and the tail-wagging dogs. Few people can pass such large and friendly animals and not even glance at them, especially when they were about to pass less than ten feet apart. Luke wavered back and forth between speaking up and keeping his silence, sure that at any moment she would look over and he could at least say hello.

The road on the left that winds up to the top of the cemetery is where Luke Conroy first saw the young woman. She turned left, walking straight toward him. Luke points to the spot where they passed.

But the young woman continued her fixed stare and walked right by him and the dogs. Luke's initial reaction at this extreme cold shoulder treatment was, "I can't believe she dissed me like that!" He immediately became determined to speak to her, and taking no more than two steps since she had passed, turned around.

The woman was nowhere in sight. Luke stood for a moment in total disbelief, thinking that not even an Olympic sprinter could have gotten out of sight in the span of a single second.

Several large trees were spaced along the road, and even though he couldn't believe a grown person would suddenly hide behind a tree, he and the dogs ran the few paces across the road to the trees. No one was there. He went back and forth among the trees and along the road searching for an answer. There was none. Somehow, a woman that both he and the dogs had clearly seen, and that he could describe with such detail as to notice her brown hair blowing in the wind, had simply vanished in a split second. He had seen her for a total of a couple of minutes, saw her walking as clearly and as naturally as any living person. Unlike a living being, however, this "woman" had the ability vanish into thin air.

The incident obviously shook him, and even relating the story a year later it is clear that the apparition of the young woman has left a lasting impression on him. Trying to find some reason behind this frightening and fascinating incident, I asked whether the area of the cemetery where he first saw the young woman had any special significance or activity. He replied that it wasn't any more or less strange than the rest of the place. Thinking for a moment, I then asked if there had been any recent burials in that area around the time of her appearance.

An unusual expression came over Luke's face as he remembered that the area of the cemetery where he first noticed the woman had indeed been the location of a recent burial—the burial of a young woman in her twenties. In fact, it had been one of the most difficult burials he had ever attended. The young woman had died suddenly, leaving a devastated husband, friends and relatives. Despite this unnerving revelation, Luke did not have the heart to now ask the grief-stricken family about how the woman had looked when she was alive. That would have raised questions that would only have upset her relatives even more.

Another bizarre incident in the cemetery left an impression of a different kind, an impression on photographic film. The Receiving Tomb is a structure built into the side of the hill and is used to temporarily store some caskets before burial. Several years ago, the wooden door of the tomb needed to be replaced. A couple of workmen installed the new door and then took pictures in order to show that their work had been completed.

When the film was developed, one of photos showed a small, white baby's casket sitting on the road near the tomb. Both men were stunned; they were absolutely positive no casket was in the road when they took the picture. Also, several photos had been taken at the same time, just a few seconds apart, yet in only one did the baby's casket appear.

The Receiving Tomb

It is perhaps not a coincidence that the area directly across from the Receiving Tomb is the location of the old baby cemetery. Also, as Nancy explained, baby caskets are extremely fragile and are *never* placed inside a Receiving Tomb. And, of course, no one would ever even *think* of leaving a baby casket unattended in the middle of the road. There is absolutely no rational explanation for this casket to have appeared in a photo of the

Receiving Tomb.

While there is certainly ample fuel for hauntings in the abode of the dead, the situation at Oak Hill may actually have been exacerbated by the actions of the living. Not one, but *two* former caretakers committed suicide on the property. One man shot himself in the basement of the caretaker's house, while the other shot himself on the hill amongst the tombstones. Is there something in this cemetery that could drive a person to such a desperate act, or was it merely an incredible coincidence?

Whatever the case may have been, it did not make it any easier when it came time for Luke to tell Nancy about his new job. As if living and working in a cemetery wasn't unsettling enough, he had to explain that two people who previously held this job killed themselves. Even if you are not superstitious, such a record has to make you stop and think.

It was a sunny March day when I went to visit Luke at Oak Hill Cemetery. Molly and Daisy formed my welcoming committee, and I instantly found it hard to believe that anyone could ignore such friendly dogs. Luke retraced his steps of the day he saw the vanishing woman. Pointing out where he was in relation to the mysterious figure at all times during the encounter, it was clear that it must have been a very prolonged sighting, regardless of whether he realized it as such at the time.

The paved road upon which she walked is rather narrow, and at the point where they passed, Luke was almost close enough to have been able to reach out and touch her. It is impossible to think that the woman did not see Luke and his dogs. And it is clearly not in the realm of possibility that any living human being could have gotten out of sight in what amounted to not much more than the blink of an eye. Even if for some bizarre reason she had suddenly decided to jump behind a tree, there would be nowhere to go from there without being seen. Based upon all the facts, the mysterious young woman of Oak Hill Cemetery is one of the most convincing sightings I've investigated.

I scanned much of the cemetery and the house with the EMF meter, but did not encounter so much as a blip that day. The only tense moment came in the basement, which is a classic, creepy, old house basement, made all the creepier by the knowledge that someone had tragically ended his life there. I was walking slowly back and forth with the meter, when Luke was called away by a phone call. Moments after I was left alone down there, the meter began to display unnaturally high readings, but not nearly as high as the level of goose bumps that suddenly appeared on my arms.

As one foot moved forward to investigate, the other was tempted to head for the stairs. Taking a deep breath, I leaned forward toward the wall, trying not to let the image of the suicide victim get the better of my imagination. The creaking floorboards from the people walking upstairs above me certainly didn't help matters. The readings continued to rise as I approached the wall, until they went far beyond the supernatural range. With a sigh of relief, I looked behind the pipes on the wall in front of me, and found that the electrical lines to the house came in at that spot, and it was this natural electricity that had created the readings on the meter. Still, I was glad to get out of the basement.

Are there restless spirits of the dead roaming the grounds of Oak Hill Cemetery? A skeptic would say no, that only mankind's overactive imagination is at work here. Yet, did the camera play tricks when it captured the image of the baby's casket? Were Luke's dogs imagining things when they reacted to the young woman who passed within a few feet? If you combine all the evidence from years of eyewitnesses, even the most hardened skeptic must admit that seeing can sometimes be believing.

As in all cases, it is up to the individual to weigh the facts and come to his own conclusion. And if you would like some firsthand experience with Oak Hill Cemetery, a guided tour is offered in the spring and autumn. While the ghosts of Oak Hill may not be famous, many of the people buried there are, and it is worth a visit to learn their fascinating history. The view of the river from the heights of the cemetery is also spectacular, and well worth the walk.

Just remember, if you do visit Oak Hill Cemetery, keep your eyes open. That child darting behind the gravestone, or the woman who just walked right by you may not be as they appear. And if you see someone standing there with a strange expression, take care, for he might have just seen a ghost. Or, perhaps he is one.

***

In January of 2001, I presented a lecture on "The Ghosts of Nyack" at the Nyack Library. The coordinator of the event was Bob Goldberg, the historian who conducts the tours of Oak Hill Cemetery.

At the conclusion of my talk (in which I related this story), Bob told me that years ago when he was about to give the first tour of the cemetery, he had mixed feelings about it. As he stood at the entrance with the tour group, he wondered if a cemetery was a proper place to give a tour, even though there was so much fascinating history to be learned from it.

Finally deciding that there was nothing wrong with the idea, he signaled the start of the tour and the group moved forward. Immediately a massive branch from a tree directly in front of them came crashing down. No one was hurt, but it was a close call.

Although Bob thought nothing of it at the time, one can hardly help but wonder if the restless spirits of Oak Hill Cemetery were particularly agitated that day.

DOWN ON THE FARM

If you have ever lived and worked on a farm you know how attached you can become to the land that provides for you and your family. It's only natural that it's often very difficult for farmers to leave their land, no matter what the reason. However, if that reason is death, then it is completely unnatural if they still remain.

This seems to have been the case with an old farmhouse on Gibson Road in Goshen, New York. In the late 1970s, a family from the deep South had moved to Goshen and were happy to find the old farm and make it their home. They have since moved away, so the information for this story came from their friends, a Mrs. H. and her daughter Lisa. Before buying the house, the family was not aware that the place had a reputation for being haunted. However, it didn't take them long to discover that fact for themselves, as it was only a week after moving in that they began experiencing bizarre phenomena.

Mrs. H. and Lisa first witnessed the inexplicable events one night when they were visiting. Everyone was sitting in the living room talking and watching television. No one was in the kitchen, but all of a sudden they heard the washing machine turn itself on. At the same moment, there was also the sound of metal objects being thrown about. They all ran into the kitchen and saw that the silverware was scattered around the room, as if it had been thrown by unseen hands. Perhaps these same phantom hands had started the washing machine.

As strange as this all was, since no one actually saw anything happen, there was a tacit agreement to try to ignore the whole incident and hope it would never happen again.

They were to have no such luck. A few nights later, Lisa and her mother were in the barn with one of the owners' sons, Roger. Roger happened to look back toward the house and there on the roof was an elderly man clad in overalls! No doubt wondering not only why this old man was up on their roof, but how on earth he got there, they all ran towards the house. As they got close, the old man simply disappeared. All three witnesses agree that he didn't climb down, go through a window or leave that roof by any conventional means—he simply disappeared before their eyes.

There was an even more disconcerting otherworldly phenomena that took place at the old farm. The house still had its original dirt floor cellar, a cellar that used to be the slaves' quarters. Horrible reminders of this awful past history of the house still hung against the walls—chains and shackles that once bound these poor souls to their dark and

106

dirty prison. Much to the family's dismay, often at night they could clearly hear the distinct and unnerving sounds of the shackles knocking against the walls of the cellar. There were no windows or doors open down there to create a breeze strong enough to even rattle the chains, let alone create the loud and eerie banging sound they all heard.

The elderly man in the overalls who was seen on the roof, was also seen inside the house. Several witnesses watched in disbelief as he went up the staircase, not walking step-by-step, but floating above it. Curiosity and courage enabled them follow, but when he reached the second floor he once again vanished into thin air. (Perhaps they should have gone outside and checked the roof?)

On another occasion, Mrs. H. and Lisa were visiting their friends when they all saw three men in a small boat on the pond. Amazed that these trespassers had the nerve to go boating on their property in full view of everyone, Roger and his brother ran toward the pond to confront the men. As with all of the previous apparitions, as soon as these ghosts realized they were being pursued, they simply vanished, boat and all.

The apparitions and sounds continued, and the family eventually moved away. After surviving for generations, the old farmhouse was torn down. The pond is still there, so if you drive by and see three men in a boat, you just might want to stop the car and take a picture. Even though the house is gone, the spirits of the farmer, the boaters and the slaves may still cling to that spot. They may be waiting for new houses to be built on the site, so that they can continue their appearances and chain-rattling activity.

If you hear strange noises in your brand new house, perhaps you ought to take the time to find out what was on the land before your place was built. You may just discover that your new house is actually a ghost's old haunting grounds.

**

Since writing of this story, several new houses have been built around the pond. I wonder if anyone there has seen a man on their roof, or heard chains rattling in their basement?

PEACH GROVE INN

While English cuisine often seems to be a contradiction in terms, the island nation has bequeathed to the food world a wonderful legacy—high tea. Long before it became trendy, several of my friends and I sought out places to have tea in New York City, as well as on our travels in Europe. We dubbed ourselves the "Sconeheads," and have actually become quite competent in creating our own high teas, from the little cucumber and dill sandwiches to the fancy pastries.

As my birthday approached in March of 2000, my fellow Sconehead, Pauline Kranick, told me that she saw an ad in the paper for a high tea being served at the Peach Grove Inn, in Warwick, New York. It sounded like a great place to have a birthday celebration, so one bright, early spring Sunday, Pauline, her husband Jim, Bob Strong and I put on our tea clothes and went to the Inn.

The Peach Grove Inn on Route 17A in Warwick is one of those houses that you drive by and think, "If I ever win the lottery I'm going to get myself a house like that!" Built in 1850 by Colonel Wheeler, it is a stately structure with white columns, four chimneys, and magnificent architectural details. Upon entering, it is like stepping back into another era. Owners John and Lucy Mastropierro have lovingly restored the interior to its 19th century splendor and began operating it as a bed and breakfast in the early 90s. While some bed and breakfasts go overboard and get a little too cutesy in their decorating, John and Lucy have used nothing but simple, elegant, pure good taste.

The original house built by Col. Wheeler.

The four of us were seated in the back parlor, while a couple occupied the table in the adjacent front parlor. The food was fabulous, and we probably all ate more than we should have. While speaking with John about the history of the house, I couldn't resist asking if there were any ghosts. I never know what kind of reaction I will get from such a question, but John honestly replied that he and Lucy had never seen anything, but some guests and former residents had. The conversation soon centered on ghosts, with Lucy and the other couple joining in. Fascinated by what they had to say, I decided to return two days later to record the full story.

Arriving at 10 am on a chilly, gray, rainy Tuesday, I sat with John and Lucy in the dining room and we discussed both the history of the house and the hauntings. They repeated the fact that in the eleven years that they have owned the house they have not heard or seen anything. They also did not have any reason to suspect that the house into which they were moving might not be empty.

In retrospect, they now find it curious that the man from whom they bought the property said only one thing to them at the closing, that they would "find the house very friendly." Soon after moving in, they began to hear bits and pieces of stories about possible hauntings, and of the death of a 16-year-old girl in the house in

The Peach Grove Inn today.

the 1800s, as well as an early 20th century suicide. One elderly ex-resident who came to visit her old home told them that even though they might hear stories, none of them were true. In fact, she was quite adamant that absolutely no kind of otherworldly activity *ever* took place in the house. Perhaps this was a case of her protesting too much?

The Mastropierro's daughter, who was in her late 20s at the time, lived with them on several occasions. While she also never heard or saw anything, she did mention on numerous occasions that she felt that something or someone was in the house. Her dog, a Lab mix, often seemed to confirm her feeling. The dog would stare at seemingly empty space, his eyes following something only he could see. His ears would perk up at sounds beyond human range, and he would generally act as if someone or something was indeed in the house.

When another ex-resident came to visit, the conversation led to ghosts. The woman said that when she lived there with her in-laws, they occupied the upper floors, while her bedroom was on the first floor in the present-day dining room just to the right of the front entrance. The door from her bedroom to the foyer was always kept closed for privacy. Late one afternoon at a time when her mother-in-law usually arrived home, she heard the front door open (a very large wooden door that clearly makes distinctive sounds upon opening), heard the door close again and then listened to footsteps going across the foyer and up the stairs. This was followed by the sound of an upstairs bedroom door opening and closing. The woman felt no alarm at the sounds as this was the time her mother-in-law usually came home and went upstairs.

However, a few minutes later she heard the front door open again. Footsteps went across the foyer, up the stairs and then an upstairs bedroom door opened and closed a second time. Curious, she went upstairs to speak to her mother-in-law. Upon questioning her, she found that this was the first time her mother-in-law had entered the house. Explaining that just minutes before she had heard someone else enter, the older woman reassured her that she had just now arrived home and this was the first time this afternoon she was entering the house. No one else was discovered to be inside, and the mystery of the phantom intruder went unsolved.

Then in 1998, came an unsettling letter from a guest who had recently stayed at the Inn. The woman had experienced a most unusual phenomenon during the night, so unusual that fearing ridicule or embarrassment, she didn't say a word about it during breakfast the following morning and left holding her silence. However, when she returned home, she told the story to her children and they urged her to write a letter to John and Lucy explaining what had happened.

She had occupied the bedroom in the front of the house on the east side. While enjoying a peaceful sleep in the comfortable four-poster bed, she suddenly awoke in the middle of the night to see the figure of an old man standing by the left side of the bed. Even more bizarre, was the large dog who then jumped up onto the foot of her bed and either sat or laid down for a moment. The dog was so real that she actually felt the pressure of his weight on her legs. The dog then jumped down off the bed on the right side and vanished. At the same instant, the old man vanished as well.

Lucy admits to feeling somewhat unnerved while reading the letter, firstly because they did not own a dog and no elderly man was staying at the Inn at that time. In addition, the woman relayed the incident with such honest and chilling detail that it was hard not to believe every word. Also, the woman who had experienced these phantom nighttime visitors had no other reason to write the letter, other than to tell the truth. (By the way, her husband, who had been in bed next to her, slept through the entire incident. While some men are extremely sensitive, this would not be the first case on record of a husband being oblivious to the obvious!)

Naturally curious about this old man and his dog, the Mastropierros brought up the subject to a man who had once lived in the house. Rather than responding to the inquiry with laughter and skepticism, the man's reaction was quite direct and surprising. The story of the apparition of the man and the dog was nothing new in his family. In fact, the man said that if he made a few phone calls, he could probably even come up with the dog's name! There was no mention as to the identity of the ghostly old man, but perhaps that was a sensitive subject. However, it is probably safe to assume that man's best friend was still accompanying his former master even after death.

The bed on which the phantom dog makes his appearance.

In January of 2000, another guest related an unusual story, this time right after it occurred. Coming down for breakfast, he asked Lucy if she had brought any flowers into the house, or had used any type of floral perfume or air freshener that morning. When she replied that she had not, the man went on to describe that while his wife was in the bathroom of their front bedroom on the west side of the house, he experienced the very strong scent of flowers by a chair in the corner. He called his wife out of the bathroom to see if she also smelled the flowers, but in those few moments the scent had completely vanished. She assured him she had not opened any perfume or other scented material so that the floral aroma could not have come from her. Since it was the dead of winter, no windows were open, and of course, nothing would have been in bloom anyway. Once again, there was a phenomenon with no explanation.

Another incident recently occurred in the back bedroom known as the servants' quarters. A woman spending the night there swears that an unseen figure sat on her bed. She felt the weight of something settle on the bed and saw the depression as if a person was sitting there, but nothing else was visible.

Many other guests over the years have talked about creaking noises, footsteps in the attic, and other strange sounds, things that the Mastropierros always explained as simply the natural sounds of an old house. They may now want to rethink that explanation in terms of something unnatural.

After recording all of the details of these stories, I decided to take a few readings with the EMF meter. I turned the unit on, placed it on the dining room table and explained that normal background readings should be zero or 0.1, with the paranormal range being roughly 2.0 to 4.0. Not expecting to find anything in the dining room in the middle of the day, I picked up the meter and started to walk around in order to demonstrate how the readings would not change as I moved. Taking two steps towards the fireplace, the readings changed, shooting up to 2.1. Stepping back to the table to the area that had previously read zero, the meter was now also up over two. I asked if there was any kind of unusual electrical appliances or high-tension lines or anything else in the house or surrounding area that would cause these anomalous readings. No natural explanation could be found.

A few moments later, the meter went back down to zero again. A second time the readings in the room went up and then went down, as if something was passing through. Our curiosity peaked by the roving EM field, we began to explore the rest of the house. The foyer was "clean" with steady zero or 0.1 readings. The staircase also gave the same neutral results. Upon entering the room in which had appeared the ghost of the old man and dog, the readings initially held steady at zero. I placed the meter on the bed near the pillows with no result. However, when I moved it to the foot of the bed, the readings once again shot up. After slowly moving the meter back and forth several times, it appeared that for some reason an area roughly about a foot long and the width of the bed had readings in the paranormal range, while just up by the pillows it was zero. Was the ghostly dog sitting there the entire time looking for attention? If so, he certainly got ours.

Four separate times I tested that room and the bed, with the mysterious results once again coming and going as if whatever was causing the high readings was moving through the room and over the bed.

We next went into the room where the man had caught the scent of flowers. The meter held at zero, until I approached the corner where he said the flowery aroma had manifested. As if on cue, the meter shot up, and remained firmly entrenched in the paranormal activity range. A bench across the room also gave high readings. However, on a second sweep through the room there was nothing.

Moving on to the servants' quarters where the woman had claimed some invisible entity sat on the bed, we once again found high readings. These readings were only found on the right side of the bed and nowhere else in the room. And once again the bizarre readings came and went with no rational explanation.

The chair in the corner of the bedroom where
there was a strong scent of flowers.

The back bedroom next to the "flower" room, where no unusual phenomenon had ever been reported, was completely clear. Then we came to the small room in the front known as the nursery. I put the meter on the bed (it was reading 0.1) and started to talk to Lucy (John had just gotten a phone call, coincidentally from a former resident who hadn't called in ages) about possible explanations for the seemingly inexplicable occurrences. I tried to explain that the meter simply was not supposed to react like that. I have encountered readings that have come and gone, but never so many, and at so many times!

Just then, I got a little tickle on the back of my neck and I said to her, "You know, I have a feeling they are playing games with us." No sooner had those words left my lips, when the meter that was on the bed suddenly registered readings of close to three! Waving my finger in the air, I said with a laugh, "Aha! I'm on to you! I know what you're all up to!" The high readings held for a few more moments and then disappeared.

Picking up the meter, we continued to scan the rest of the house, the attic, and some of the property. The meter held steady around zero. The game was apparently over.

In its 150 years, the old Wheeler estate has most assuredly seen its share of heartaches and tragedies. It has also had the honor of being occupied by many people who grew to love the house and no doubt never wanted to leave it. It is the latter scenario that most likely accounts for the playful, generally unobtrusive ghosts that may still walk the halls and sit on the furniture of the home they knew during their lives.

While the Mastropierros and the majority of their guests have never encountered anything unusual, it is clear that a sensitive few have glimpsed these inhabitants of another world. Perhaps if you spend the night at the Inn, you will be visited by the man and his dog. Or, if you choose to attend one of their wonderful teas, a scent of flowers might pass by your table. It is also just possible, that you will see or hear something no one else has ever experienced. In any event, regardless of whether you might be entertained at the Peach Grove Inn by the friendly ghosts, you will most definitely be warmly received by the friendly hosts.

***

I was contacted by Andre, the producer of the "Woodman's" radio show on K104.7 around Halloween of 2000. He had recently become interested in ghosts and wondered if we could do a live broadcast from a haunted site. I suggested the Peach Grove Inn and a few days later we met there with two other members of the station.

It was early in the morning and with the help of John and Lucy we got the tapes rolling, meters going and began to tour the house. We almost immediately encountered the same cat and mouse (or ghost and human) game of readings coming and going. It was clear that the radio station crew was a little on edge, but who could blame them.

At one point upstairs, the man holding the microphone distinctly felt something poke him in the leg. He turned to tell his friend to cut it out because it wasn't funny, but his friend was not there. In fact, no one or no thing was anywhere near him.

Convinced that there was genuine paranormal activity in the house, Andre got on his cell phone and called into the show's host, the "Woodman" at the station. I didn't need to hear both sides of the conversation to know that Woodman did not share his producer's beliefs. When I got on the phone, it was clear that the "play everything for laughs and don't let the guest finish a sentence" DJ mentality was the order of the day, so I played along for a few minutes and was more than happy to end the phone "interview."

However, it turned out to be worth it, because a listener had a very interesting tale to tell. A woman who had stayed at the inn the night before her wedding was driving in her car, listening to the broadcast and said she "nearly drove off the road" when she heard that the inn might be haunted.

It seems that right before bed that night, she hung her wedding gown on the back of the door to her room and a few moments later she looked and saw the gown laying on the floor, with the hanger still on the door. This made no sense, as she had securely pinned the gown to the hangar. Picking

114

up the gown, she put it back on the hangar, refastened all of the pins, making sure there was no way it could come loose again, put it back on the door and went to bed. When she awoke the morning of her wedding, her gown was once again laying on the floor. It was as if someone had purposely removed all of the pins and pushed the gown off the hangar onto the floor.

While it was clearly a mystery, she had a few other things to occupy her thoughts that day and quickly forgot all about the bizarre incident. It wasn't until she was driving to work that day and heard me talking about the hauntings at the inn that she remembered the dress incident and felt that finally she had a possible explanation. But why would one of the ghosts do such a thing? Was it simply another playful prank, or did one of the restless spirits (perhaps that of the young girl who died unmarried) resent the happy event?

Another fascinating story was to surface shortly after the radio broadcast. Two young women who often help Lucy with the cleaning on the weekends are actually granddaughters of a former owner. They both remember hearing an old family story that was told on many occasions.

Late one night when the owner's son and daughter-in-law were occupying the present-day dining room on the ground floor (on the east side of the house), he was in his upstairs bedroom and heard loud voices. Coming downstairs, the doors to the parlor (on the west side of the house) were closed and he clearly heard the voices of a man and woman in a heated argument.

At first he was inclined to go into the parlor to see what was the problem, but he had never heard his son and his daughter-in-law argue in such a manner and he decided not to stick his nose into their affairs. A few moments after he had gone back upstairs he heard the front door open and then slam shut. Hurrying to a window, he saw a woman running from the house off to the west and disappearing in the darkness. Even though there wasn't much light, he was positive it was a woman, and equally positive that she was wearing a long, old-fashioned dress with a full skirt.

When morning came, the owner could not resist asking his son what had happened the night before. His son looked at him with a puzzled expression and asked what he was talking about. The owner said he had overheard their argument in the parlor and then saw his son's wife running from the house. Again the son wanted to know what in the world he was talking about.

The son and his wife did not go into the parlor that night. In fact, they never left their room. They did not have an argument. In fact, they didn't even have a conversation because at that hour they were sound asleep. They also didn't hear any voices or the front door (which is just a few feet from their door) opening and slamming. The son made it abundantly clear that if two people were arguing in the middle of the night and a woman in an old dress ran from the house, he knew nothing about it.

The most recent occurrence was in the servant's quarters room at the back of the house, the same room where an unseen figure sat on the bed. This time the spirit was apparently in a more amorous mood, because another woman who slept there (who knew nothing of the hauntings) came down to breakfast the next morning and announced that she would swear that someone kissed her cheek during the night. No one else was in the room, but she distinctly felt the kiss.

I'm sure the Peach Grove Inn has many more fascinating tales to tell, but hopefully the wandering spirits will realize some day that it is about time they checked out and moved on.

A MICKEY MOUSE HAUNTING

Just when I think I've heard everything, someone comes along with a story that truly pushes the spiritual envelope. If this eyewitness had not been so credible I would not be relating this story now. However, it is not for me to judge how a ghost wants to represent itself, so I will simply tell the story and let the reader be the judge.

This incident took place in one of the scariest spots on the planet, the dentist's office. If given the choice between facing a screaming apparition and root canal work, many people would give careful thought before answering. But we will leave the horrors of the dentist's chair and drill to the world of the living and instead focus on what must be one of the most bizarre displays by the dead.

It was 1961, and "Margaret Whitman" worked for a very successful dentist in Larchmont, NY. The office was in a beautiful home built in the 1850s and had three spacious floors plus an attic and basement, allowing for more than enough room for the dentist to both live and work in the old house. In all the time she worked there, Margaret only had a chance to see the first floor that held the offices. Then one summer, the dentist was going away on an extended vacation and offered her the use of the house.

Naturally curious about the upper floors, Margaret decided to take a look around. While the 100-year-old structure needed a little sprucing up, it was still full of beautiful architectural details that would make the place a real showcase once the dentist's planned renovations took place. Having worked in the house for several years without incident, Margaret had no fear while exploring the nooks and crannies of the old house, even though she was alone. Absolutely nothing unusual happened, until she began to climb the third-floor stairs that led to the attic.

The stairwell had no windows and just large plain walls surrounding it. As Margaret placed her foot on the first step, an image suddenly sprang to life on the wall to her right, just inches away. It was not the hideous face of some demon or specter, nor was it the bare-toothed grin of a skull. In Margaret's words it looked most like "people in an old Mickey Mouse cartoon being projected on the wall."

There was no sound to accompany this ghostly cartoon, and the animated figures (in full color, no less) just danced and swayed in silence. Having no idea what was going on, Margaret looked around for some explanation for the seemingly projected figures, but there was nothing but solid walls. Nowhere could she see any kind of light source and passing her hand directly in front of the images did not disrupt them. For all her education, common sense, and reason, she could find no explanation why these bizarre apparitions played along the wall of the stairway. Finally realizing this was no trick or practical joke, Margaret beat a hasty retreat.

Several days later, she found the courage to approach the third-floor staircase once again. The time that had elapsed from the first encounter no doubt gave her time to think that it had simply been some quirk of her imagination, although why her imagination would choose 1930s animation to express itself was also beyond her comprehension. Margaret was not prone to hallucinations and not only had she never believed in ghosts, she never even gave much thought to anything in that realm.

Now, however, as she approached the staircase, her heart beat a little faster. Before her was nothing but a darkened stairway, and she hoped it would remain that way. But once again, as she returned to the spot where she had seen the first spirited cartoon, the show began. There was light, there was color, and it was two-dimensional, exactly as though a projector was shining these figures on the wall of the stairwell.

Was there something in the attic that did not want her up there, and so created this bizarre show to stop her? Or, was there a playful spirit who decided to develop this very unique form of haunting? However you look at it, Margaret's experiences were truly one-of-a-kind.

When the dentist returned from vacation, Margaret said nothing of the animated apparitions. She thought it best to keep her silence, and therefore keep her job. Of course, she could not help but wonder if the dentist had also seen this incredible show, and was simply too embarrassed to mention it to her for fear of ridicule. We will never know. And we will also never know the source of this inexplicable phenomenon, for once the renovations had taken place, the cartoon shows came to an end.

How can we even begin to explain such a sight—phantom cartoon people dancing along a wall leading to an old attic? What message was trying to be conveyed, and what was in the attic? As explanations escape us, all we can do is chalk up this Mickey Mouse haunting as one for the record books.

BUT DOES THE GHOST
DO WINDOWS ?

(Although I strongly believe that no haunting is a good haunting, even I might consider inviting this ghost into my home!)

A young couple moved into a large Victorian home in Putnam County, NY. Soon after settling in, they began hearing unusual sounds, the basic "things that go bump in the night," but just chalked it up to normal old house sounds. But then something began occurring that they could not explain away. It didn't have to do with cold spots, terrible odors or terrifying apparitions. It had to do with towels.

Neither the husband nor the wife were obsessively clean, and would often leave their towels in a heap on the bathroom floor. Upon returning to the bathroom after some time, one or the other would notice that the towels were neatly folded and hanging on their racks. The husband thought the wife was just cleaning up after him, as usual, while the wife assumed that the husband had turned over a new leaf and was folding the towels himself. When the subject of the neatly folded towels came up one day, both realized to their amazement that neither one had been folding them!

However, if this was some kind of manifestation of a haunting, neither one was complaining.

Then something even more bizarre and helpful started occurring. Tired from their long days of work, the couple would often leave their dirty dishes in the sink overnight. One morning they entered the kitchen to find that all the dishes had been washed and stacked neatly in the drainer. The stunned husband and wife were both willing to swear on a stack of Bibles that neither of them had washed those dishes.

When these mysterious and spontaneous cleaning events continued to occur throughout the house, their curiosity reached a fever pitch. There was obviously someone or something else in their house, someone who obviously disapproved of their housekeeping skills, or lack thereof. Even though they came to firmly believe that the folded towels and washed dishes were some kind of manifestation of a haunting, still neither one was complaining. But they did want some answers.

They sought out an elderly man who lived in the house for many years, a well-educated Reverend who still had a residence in town. Hesitant to sound foolish, they casually tried to ask if anyone that he had known who lived there was particular about cleanliness. The old Reverend smiled knowingly, and didn't hesitate to tell them he knew exactly what they were going through and who was behind it.

The Reverend's grandfather had been a stickler for neatness and order. Despite having lost an arm, his grandfather insisted that everything should be clean and in its place, and often did household chores himself. Although the Reverend is a learned man of the cloth, he has no doubt that granddad has neither left his house nor changed his obsessively neat habits.

The couple was relieved to hear the news, and took no further steps in their ghost investigation. They did not call in an exorcist or a psychic to try to end the haunting of the ghost who often did their dishes and tidied up the place. They did not burn candles and say prayers to drive the spirit from the house. But then, in an era when it's so hard to find good help, who would?

PRESIDENTS AND PANCAKES- THE UNIQUE HAUNTINGS OF LINDENWALD

The Hudson Valley is filled with historical treasures, and it is always a delight to research and write about them. If these places also happen to be extremely haunted, we get the extra bonus of being able to delve into both worlds.

One of the historic jewels of the region is the mansion of Lindenwald in Kinderhook in Columbia County, NY. It had been the home of a president, a suicidal butler, and a tyrannical cook, any or all of who may still walk the halls and grounds. It is a place of great history, as well as a place of great mystery, and worthy of serious exploration by scholar and paranormal researcher alike.

The town of Kinderhook was an early Dutch settlement and its name means "children's corner." It was a favorite haunt (of the living variety) of Washington Irving, and it was Kinderhook's local teacher upon whom he based the famous character of Ichabod Crane. Irving also drew inspiration from other people and places in Kinderhook for his famous *Legend of Sleepy Hollow*.

The town is also known as the birthplace of the 8th president of the United States, Martin Van Buren, who was born there in 1782. He was to return to Kinderhook after he left the White House, but there is a little more history to fill in before we attend to the president.

119

Lindenwald

Lindenwald was built by Judge William Peter Van Ness in the year 1797. The structure began life as a more modest brick Dutch farmhouse, but would see extensive remodeling and expansion over the years. The son of the original builder, William "Billy" Van Ness, gained some fame, or infamy as the case may be, when he acted as the second for former Vice-President Aaron Burr. The duel in question was the tragic episode that resulted in Burr killing Alexander Hamilton. Hamilton's death deprived the young American nation of one of its truly great and dynamic intellectuals. It also turned up the heat under an already unpopular Aaron Burr who sought to drop out of sight until things cooled down.

For many years, it was suspected that after the murder of Hamilton, Burr fled to Lindenwald where he was to hide out for three years. Supposed evidence of this was the discovery of a secret, windowless room, in the early 1900s. While the roof was being replaced, the secret room was revealed and the owner, one Dr. Birney, somewhat ungallantly lowered his own daughter into the dark room, suspended on a rope, to investigate. According to Dr. Birney, the room was empty except for three items, a small toy pig, a little rocking chair and Aaron Burr's personal calling card.

This flimsy "proof" of the presence of Burr's calling card did not hold up to scrutiny. As tempting as it is to imagine Burr hiding for three years in this dark, secret room, it turns out that this room had not even been built during the time of his alleged stay at Lindenwald. However, even though presently there is no evidence to substantiate these earlier claims, the ghost of Aaron Burr has nonetheless been spotted several times. Eyewitnesses describe Burr, wearing a maroon-colored coat and lace ruffles that *did not* move in the breeze, walking slowly through the orchard. Unfortunately, the orchard no longer exists, but the National Parks system does have plans to restore it. Perhaps when the trees are growing again, Burr will resume his midnight walks.

The ghost of President Martin Van Buren has also been spotted at Lindenwald. After having served as president of the United States, Van Buren retired and decided to move back to Kinderhook. He was a friend of the Van Ness family and was familiar with their home at Lindenwald and decided that it was there he wanted to spend his remaining years. Van Buren was able to persuade Billy Van Ness to sell the house and the ex-president soon made it his home. Calling upon Richard Upjohn, the architect for Trinity Church in New York City, Van Buren ordered extensive remodeling and expansion. Inside and out, Lindenwald became a showplace of wealth and refinement. Yet, despite the time and energy Van Buren poured into the house, it is also in the orchard that his ghost was most often seen.

This apple orchard must have been a spiritual hot spot, for another of Lindenwald's shadowy apparitions made its appearances there. Van Buren apparently had in his employ a butler who seemed to make liberal use of the contents of the liquor cabinet. Whether from an alcohol-induced depression, or for some other unknown reason, the unhappy butler chose to hang himself from one of the apple trees. While the orchard was still standing, witnesses claimed to see the figure of the dead butler swinging in one of the trees.

A more recent ghost was also glimpsed on the mansion grounds. In the middle of the 20th century, there were reports that a woman had been murdered near Lindenwald's gatehouse, and the poor victim's white apparition has been seen in the vicinity ever since.

While few properties can boast such famous spirits as the ghost of a president and the murderer of Alexander Hamilton, the house itself is not to be outdone. Several generations of private owners have heard footsteps and slamming doors when no one else was in the house. As for the doors themselves, they are massive, made of solid wood and are mounted on sturdy hinges. It is unlikely that such doors would open and close on their own. And while creaking floorboards can be expected in such an old house, eyewitnesses insist that the sounds were clearly those of *footsteps*, not creaking wood.

One theory as to originator of these footsteps involves the son of Martin Van Buren. "Prince" John Van Buren was a spoiled, hard drinking gambler. Legend has it that his father had to fill in the fishpond that was on the estate because his drunken son too often fell into it. After his father passed away,

The foundation of the original gatehouse where a white apparition is seen.

Prince John continued his dissolute lifestyle and actually ended up losing the Lindenwald mansion in a card game! (In an interesting twist, he had also bet his mistress along with the house, but history does not record whether she honored his gambling debt.) Some people believe that Prince John still walks the corridors and slams the doors of the home he loved, and so abruptly and foolishly lost.

The lucky card player who won Lindenwald was a man by the name of Leonard Jerome from New York City. Jerome owned several properties in the area, and it is doubtful whether he actually resided at Lindenwald. While none of the Jerome family is suspected of haunting the house and grounds, it is worth mentioning them because of one of the daughters, Jennie. As was the fashion in those days, Jennie was sent to England, ostensibly to learn culture and refinement, but more likely to snag a wealthy and influential husband.

In the latter regard her trip was a great success, and one that was to play a major role in the history of the world. Jennie Jerome was able to catch the eye of an English aristocrat and they were married. This daughter of a former owner of Lindenwald gave birth to a son. This boy was none other than Winston Churchill, a man who steadfastly led his nation out of its darkest hour. Perhaps some of his spunk had been derived from his New York gambler grandfather. In any event, it is just one more interesting piece of history that makes this region so fascinating.

Getting back to the ghosts, we come across the unusual and amusing character of Aunt Sarah. There are unsubstantiated reports that the skeletons of 15 slaves are buried in the wine cellar, although Van Buren himself did not own slaves. However, there were many free African-Americans in the area, and several were on Lindenwald's staff during his years there, according to a former Director of the NYS Historical Association. The most memorable was Aunt Sarah, the cook, who ruled her basement kitchen as a sovereign territory, not to be trespassed by anyone. Whenever it was necessary for someone else to enter her domain, the visit was always brief and with her consent.

Such dictatorial behavior was no doubt tolerated because Aunt Sarah was a cook of extraordinary abilities. But as all good things must end, after many years of producing fabulous breakfasts, lunches and dinners, Aunt Sarah passed away. However, it is just possible that not even death could keep the talented but ornery Aunt Sarah from attending to her duties in the kitchen.

For several years in the long history of Lindenwald, the house was vacant. A nearby neighbor, a Mrs. Wagner, took it upon herself to keep an eye on the house and property. When she was informed that new owners were planning to move in, she instructed her servant, Tom, to clean up the kitchen and get ready for the new residents. Tom was reluctant, to say the least, because he had personally known Aunt Sarah and her strict rules about outsiders entering her realm. His protests fell upon deaf ears, however, and Tom, with much trepidation, went into the basement of Lindenwald and entered Aunt Sarah's kitchen. The following is an account of what transpired in Tom's own words:

"I went down into the cellar and then into the kitchen, but the minute I took up a pan I heard a sound. As I looked up, down the chimney came Aunt Sarah. She was covered with soot, but her eyes were blazing, and the ends of her kerchief stood up on her head just like horns. So I said to myself, 'Tom, you're getting out of this cellar as fast as you can, and nobody's going to make you go back.'"

Perhaps fear and an over-active imagination fueled Tom's sighting, or perhaps Aunt Sarah (who seemed to appear more like a demon-possessed Aunt Jemima) did actually come back to defend her sacred kitchen. While there are no other reports of actual angry Aunt Sarah sightings, a kindler, gentler Aunt Sarah may have decided to make her presence known in a different manner.

Several families who have occupied Lindenwald have reported waking up in the morning to the smell of buttery, hot pancakes. While strongest in the dining room, the aroma often pervaded the entire house in the early daylight hours. Numerous people searching for the source of this enticing smell have gone down into Sarah's old kitchen,  only to find a cold and empty fireplace and griddle. One wonders whether these people were relieved not to find Sarah's ghost cooking phantom pancakes, or were disappointed that the delicious aromas were not to be followed by a hearty breakfast.

Over the course of investigations for *Ghosts of Rockland County* and *Haunted Hudson Valley*, I have heard reports of everything from the pleasant scent of a long gone perfume, to the hideous stench of phantom corpses. However, the ghostly aroma of pancakes is further evidence that in the ghost hunting game one never knows what to expect!

Naturally suspicious about such a bizarre manifestation, I was somewhat surprised when I spoke with the Supervisory Park Ranger at Lindenwald, Marion Berntson. As luck would have it, I spoke with Marion on her last day before retirement after 16 years at Lindenwald. Her very first comment to my inquiry of haunted happenings was that she and others on the staff have regularly opened the house early in the morning and have been greeted by the delectable, buttery aroma of homemade pancakes! Unless geologists can prove that there is an underground spring of batter and butter flowing beneath Lindenwald, we must bow to the overwhelming evidence provided by dozens of eyewitnesses over the course of generations; Aunt Sarah's pancakes live on!

Marion also told me that on one occasion she was locking up the house after the last tour of the day. She thought she was the only one left in the house, until she heard a female voice upstairs. Her immediate thought was that someone had lagged behind or become lost on the tour and was in danger of being locked in for the night. Calling upstairs, she received no response. Still not believing that anything out of the ordinary was going on (other than the fact that a tourist had wandered off), Marion went upstairs to find the lost soul. Apparently, a lost soul was exactly what had produced the female voice, because no one could be found.

In addition to footsteps, doors closing, and the classic cold spots, Marion Berntson and another Park Ranger encountered a very unusual phenomenon. It was around closing time when the two Rangers noticed that one of the curtains had become quite dusty and was in need of a cleaning. They decided that they would attend to this on the following day, left together and locked the door. Upon returning together the following morning, the two women entered to find that the dirty curtain was no longer hanging on the window, but was sitting in a wash basin! Had Aunt Sarah left her kitchen long enough to try to tidy up another part of the house, or had some other conscientious spirit tried to help in the household chores?

On another occasion, New Year's Eve to be exact, the house was empty and securely locked. In order to preserve the house and its valuable contents, temperature and humidity levels are constantly monitored with equipment known as hydrothermalgraphs. These units produce charts of temperature and humidity 24 hours a day. When staff members returned to Lindenwald after the New Year's holiday, they were stunned to find that on midnight of

New Year's Eve, the temperature suddenly rose inside the house, almost as if warm-blooded people were partying in the new year. After several hours of this inexplicable spike in degrees, the temperature had returned itself to normal levels and no explanation for the sudden warming was ever found.

Always interested in maintaining the historical integrity of a site, National Park researchers found that a portrait of Lady Wellington was once over the mantle in one of the rooms at Lindenwald. Lady Wellington had been a friend of Van Buren's daughter, Angelica, and it was Angelica's portrait that now hung over this mantle. With the assistance of another Park Ranger, Marion planned to remove Angelica's portrait and replace it with that of Lady Wellington. However, as it was being removed from the wall, Angelica Van Buren's portrait suddenly left their hands and flipped completely around in the air. Startled and perplexed, they decided to put Angelica's portrait back and leave well enough alone.

Such goings on over the many years convinced Marion Berntson that Lindenwald was indeed haunted. Determined to get some hard evidence, Marion and a fellow Ranger decided to spend the night. They were prepared to come face to face with the many spirits that haunted the house and grounds. The minutes ticked by in the darkened house as they awaited the appearance of apparitions, or the sounds of footsteps, the opening and closing of doors, or voices. However, weary from a long day of work, the two women fell fast asleep and slept soundly and undisturbed right through until morning. If only ghosts kept more reasonable hours!

The National Park system did not acquire Lindenwald until 1976. Prior to that the home was always in private hands. Some families lived there for decades and heard and saw absolutely nothing unusual. Other families had enough bizarre experiences to fill an entire book.

One such family occupied Lindenwald from the early part of the 20th century until 1957. Both adults and children alike had many stories to tell of the sounds of footsteps, doors closing, the shutters banging on still nights, unseen figures leaning on their beds and the phantom strains of violin music playing in an empty room. One night one of the daughters heard the bureau drawers in the next room opening and closing repeatedly. She went into the room where another girl was spending the night, only to find the girl fast asleep and the bureau drawers closed. She awakened the girl, who clearly knew nothing of the sounds, and they went back to the daughter's room. Again, the sounds of the bureau drawers opening and closing could clearly be heard, but when they returned to the room where the sounds were coming from there was silence once again.

One of the men in the family chalked up all of these experiences to "women's nerves," as he, himself, had never experienced anything unusual and scoffed at their stories. However, late one night, there was the persistent sound of footsteps and after numerous investigations turned up no one, this firm unbeliever got a case of his own "nerves" and promptly left the house in the middle of the night. (It is always amusing to see how quickly skeptics can become believers.) Over the generations, many guests intending to spend the night have also suddenly gotten up and fled the house.

As always, I recommend that readers explore these sites themselves. If you are sensitive to things from the other world, you just might glimpse an ex-president and vice-president, smell the pancakes of a former cook, or hear the sounds that defy rational explanation. However, if you are in the category of those who could not see a ghost if it was sitting right on your lap, you should still visit Lindenwald. The tour will not only reveal the magnificent art and architecture, but will detail the fascinating lives of the unique characters who, one way or another, have left their mark on the haunted and historic Hudson Valley.

BROTHERLY LOVE

"Victor" was very close to his older brother, "Joey," even though they were separated by more than ten years. So it was difficult for Victor to understand when his parents told him that Joey wouldn't be coming home anymore.

There had been a tragic high school football accident, and Joey had received a fatal head injury. His parents tried to gently explain the realities of life and death to the young boy. They tried to explain why Joey would never be coming home again. Despite their seemingly sound reasoning, however, they could never imagine that Joey would try to come home one more time.

The family lived in Yonkers, and their house sat at the base of a hill that contained a large cemetery. There was some comfort in the fact that their son would rest in eternal peace close by them in that cemetery. After the painful funeral, life slowly got back to a normal routine, and Victor eventually came to understand and accept that his brother had died.

Victor's route home from school took him past the entrance to the cemetery. One ordinary day as the boy walked home, he saw his brother Joey standing at the cemetery entrance, looking as real and alive as he had ever been in life. Without a word, Joey approached, smiled gently and took his little brother's hand.

Quietly they walked hand and hand toward their house. Although Victor knew his brother was dead, he was not frightened, but understandably he moved along in a kind of a daze. As the two brothers entered the gate and started up the path to their house, their mother happened to look out the window.

In panicked horror, she shouted, "Joey, Joey, no!"

The apparition of her dead son stopped, and silently vanished into thin air.

If one was to just hear the story of the little boy claiming to see his big brother, it would be easy to say it was a combination of grief and imagination. But the mother instantly recognized her own son, and fearing that he had come to take Victor away, shouted out in fear. One can't blame her, losing one son is more than enough for any mother to bear, but one can not help wondering what would have transpired had she not yelled.

Joey never returned to the house, and Victor never again saw him. Hopefully, the teenager whose life was tragically cut short is now resting in peace. Somehow, Joey's love for his family enabled him to return and take the hand of his dear baby brother one more time. As Victor now enters his golden years, he is perhaps comforted in knowing that someone will be waiting for him on the other side.

AX MURDER

This is not a local tale of haunting, but it involves a Hudson Valley resident, and it is so terrifying I think you will agree it was too good to pass up.

Willets, California is about as far across the country from the Hudson Valley as you can get. However, that is probably a good thing, considering the gruesome events that occurred there a century ago, and the terrible evil which may still dwell there today.

In the 1980s "Grace," a Hudson Valley resident, received a job offer near this quiet community in the heavily wooded regions of northern California. Events moved quickly, and she soon found herself in town with only temporary housing arrangements. Affordable apartments were not easy to come by, and Grace began to wonder if she had made the right decision accepting this job and moving without more planning.

As she was beginning to feel the twinge of desperation, a woman told her about a beautiful Victorian home for rent. Grace was about to explain that she could not possibly afford such a place, when the woman finished her

127

description by adding that the rent was less than $200 per month. Assuming the house was actually a dilapidated hovel, Grace was nonetheless tempted by the attractive rent and she arranged with a realtor to view the house.

When the realtor's car pulled up in front of the house, Grace could not believe they had the right address. It was indeed a beautiful Victorian structure and in excellent condition. There was more than enough room, the location was ideal, and the price was just too good to be true. She signed on the spot. However, there is that old saying which goes, "If something appears too good to be true, it probably is." Grace should have heeded that warning. It would have saved her from the horror she was to about to undergo.

The front door opened to a spacious foyer, with a parlor to the right and a large, beautifully carved staircase climbing to a landing, then reversing direction up to the second floor. One evening, soon after moving in, Grace was relaxing in the parlor, no doubt wondering how she had been so lucky as to acquire such a place. These pleasant thoughts were soon transformed to terror by the sounds of footsteps rushing down the hall on the floor above her, and then heading down the staircase.

Frozen with fear, Grace expected to see her intruders appear on the landing at any second. However, nothing appeared—at least nothing the human eye could detect. Yet still the pair of running footsteps continued down the second half of the staircase, stairs that were in full view of Grace from her seat in the parlor. The first set of footsteps were light, like those of a woman. They were accompanied by a rustling sound of the type that would be made by the long skirts and petticoats of Victorian women. Close behind were the heavy footsteps of a man, and the odd swishing sound of something going through the air.

When the running footsteps reached the bottom of the staircase, all the sounds stopped. However, it was not a reassuring silence, as it was accompanied by a sickly stench that suddenly filled the entire parlor. A strong sense of an evil presence swept through the room and Grace ran out. Yet, as soon as she crossed the threshold into the foyer, the odor and presence vanished. Still curious despite the terrifying occurrence, Grace took a step back into the parlor. The nauseating smell of death hung heavily in the air, but seemed unable to leave that room.

As a professional trying to establish a reputation in her new town, it is perfectly understandable that Grace decided not to mention this bizarre episode to her colleagues and new friends. However, her reluctance to speak had no effect on the reoccurrence of the awful sounds and smells that continued to plague her.

The scenario always played out the same way—a woman's desperate footsteps quickly followed by a man's, the rustling skirt, the odd swishing sound and then silence at the bottom of the stairs. Then there was the stench, the horrible stench that pervaded every corner of the parlor and seeped into the upholstery and curtains, and drove her from the room. And the evil—a fearful presence which filled the house and quickly made life in that seemingly tranquil Victorian home unbearable.

Grace managed to stay for three months for the sake of the rent. However, she soon came to the inescapable conclusion that it was not worth staying there another day, even if they paid her to do it. Hastily moving all her belongings onto the front yard, she was happy to find that the stench did not remain with the items from the parlor. There was a tremendous sense of freedom and relief. There was also one other nagging emotion—just a bit of anger at the realtor who neglected to disclose the house's hidden features.

"Now that I'm out," Grace said confronting the realtor, "tell me the truth about this house."

"Well..." the realtor began with some hesitance, "the house might be haunted."

"No kidding!" Grace replied (or stronger words to that effect).

Finally, the realtor relented and told the entire gruesome story. Sometime near the turn of the century, the man who owned the house became filled with a murderous rage for reasons we may never know. Grabbing an ax, he chased his terrified wife down the hall of the second floor. Literally running for her life, she raced down the stairs, her heavy skirts rustling loudly in the effort. Just steps behind her was her husband, frantically swinging the ax at her, creating that distinctive swishing sound as it missed its target and cut through the air.

As his wife reached the bottom of the stairs, he didn't miss. The husband brutally murdered his wife with the ax, swinging again and again until her screams were silenced. Dragging her lifeless body across the foyer, he pulled her into the parlor. He then took a rope, tied it to the ceiling and hung himself. It was several days before the bodies were discovered.

The history of the brutal murder-suicide fit precisely with the otherworldly events Grace had experienced—the path of the footsteps, the rustling and swishing sounds, the deathly silence as the fatal act was consummated at the last step, and the horrible smell of corpses waiting to be found. Was Grace simply sensitive to the spectral imprint of the ghastly tragedy, or is there an even more horrifying explanation?

Perhaps the ghostly couple is doomed to repeat the awful scene throughout eternity. Is the lost soul of the wife running desperately to regain a life cut short one hundred years ago, while the spirit of the husband, still swinging a phantom ax, is so consumed with rage that he can never find peace? These questions may have been answered, except for the fact that the stately Victorian house mysteriously burned to the ground several years later.

This may have released the trapped spirits, or they could be forever locked to the site, waiting for a new house to be built on the property. If such a house is ever built, hopefully the realtor will be merciful enough to suggest a nice ranch—a simple one level home with no staircases.

Book Four

FORT DECKER

In November of 2000, I got an e-mail from Mike Worden in Port Jervis, NY. Mike is a police officer, and by coincidence, he was the third policeman who had contacted me that week about ghosts. It seems that in their line of work they literally see it all, from both the living and the dead. While Mike hadn't actually seen a ghost, he knew of a house that was reportedly very haunted and wondered if I wanted to conduct a ghost investigation for a television show that he produced for a local station.

This was no ordinary house, Mike went on to explain. In fact, it was no less than the oldest house in Port Jervis. Since the longer a house has been standing, the better the chances are for it to be haunted, I was intrigued. When Mike told me that this place was the Fort Decker stone house, originally built in 1760, it was all I needed to hear. There is something wonderful about historic sites (with or without ghosts) and the opportunity to combine history with ghost stories for a television show was an offer I couldn't refuse.

We arranged to meet at Fort Decker in early December. Since the old stone house is now a museum for the Minisink Valley Historical Society, prior to our visit I looked at their web site to get some information about the

Fort Decker

site and the area. I learned a few pertinent facts, but got the in-depth story from curator Peter Osborne.

The original stone house was built in 1760 to protect the settlers from Indian attacks. In 1779 the Mohawk Indians, led by Joseph Brandt, burned the structure. It was rebuilt in 1793 by Martinus Decker, and for a time in the 1820s it was used as a headquarters for John Jervis and the engineers who were building the Delaware and Hudson Canal. It was a private residence until 1965.

A few weeks before our meeting at Fort Decker, I purchased a new Sony camcorder with the Nightshot feature. Unlike conventional cameras that only record visible light and are useless in the dark, Nightshot technology allows you to record in infrared in complete darkness. Infrared wavelengths of light are not visible to the human eye, but ghost hunters experimenting with infrared film in their 35mm cameras obtained some fascinating results. Although no one can explain why, ghostly images, shapes and figures appear on infrared photos, even though nothing appears on regular film shot at the same time.

This exciting discovery led to the speculation that while apparitions visible to the human eye are relatively rare, there may be a wealth of spirit activity going on in the infrared range. Unfortunately, 35mm infrared film is not the easiest thing to use. It requires both special handling and developing, and the slightest mistake can lead to an expensive batch of ruined photos. The other drawback is that it only captures single frames, and while some individual photos can be impressive, there's obviously a lot you can miss in between frames, not to mention the path and speed of moving objects.

The best tool for the ghost investigator, therefore, is a camcorder that not only has the capability to see in the dark, but to see those wavelengths of light in which ghosts may dwell. Of course, Sony doesn't advertise the potential spiritual aspect of Nightshot, and sales people aren't trained to answer your ghost hunting questions. In fact, during the time I was shopping around looking for the best features and the best price, the sales people were curious, to say the least, about my interest in a camera that could film in the dark. When I said I needed Nightshot for professional reasons, the raised eyebrows indicated that their imaginations were working overtime. I didn't bother to explain further. Always keep them guessing.

We had tried the camera for the first time at the Lundy Road house (see page 171), and since there were problems (although most likely not caused by the camera) I was hoping I hadn't made an expensive mistake. This time Bob Strong would be in charge of filming. (Not only do I trust his abilities, but it gives me the option of blaming him if something does go wrong!)

We arrived at Fort Decker on a cold evening just before sunset and took a few photos of the outside of the house before knocking on the wooden front door. Peter Osborne cheerfully greeted us. There was also an unexpected guest; Amy Berkowitz of the local *Gazette* newspaper was there to cover the investigation. I was happy to have another objective observer, just in case something happened. But what were the chances of that, given the 240-year history of massacres and human tragedy?

We stood in the front hallway introducing ourselves and waiting for Mike. Peter, although definitely on the side of skepticism, began to describe some of the strange and inexplicable goings-on. For starters, even though the old stone house would be empty and locked at night, dozens of people have reported seeing the lights go on around 9pm. They would go on, staying on for as little as a few seconds, or as long as an hour, before they shut off again. Yet, how could someone be going from room to room turning the lights on and off without activating the alarms?

On other occasions, even though the house remained dark (and locked), the security alarm inside was triggered. Upon investigating these instances, no one was ever found in the house and no explanation could be found, either. After this happened a few times, the company that installed the security system was called to search for malfunctions, and to see if any adjustments to the sensitivity of the motion detectors might solve the problem. They came out on numerous occasions, but nothing helped. Both the mysterious night lights and triggering of the alarm continued.

There are also some psychics who had visited and reported all manner of strange feelings, as well as "ordinary" people who from time to time heard creaking floorboards or "felt something," but nothing tangible and convincing. There isn't anything like good "in your face" phenomena to substantiate claims of a haunting, but one could never hope to have such an occurrence on a first visit, especially within minutes of entering. Or could one?

As we listened to Peter's overview, I was standing a few feet away from a door to my left. I assumed it was a hall closet and really didn't pay any attention to it, until it started to slowly creak open on its own. As I turned to look, half of me wanted to see just another visitor or employee behind the door, while the other half hoped for something a little more dramatic. What I saw was that I was looking straight down the stairs leading to the ancient basement, and no one was there. After a moment of stunned silence, I looked back at the expressions of amazement on the faces of Bob and Amy. Peter, however, was unfazed.

"Oh, that always happens," he said shrugging it off as one of the many quirks of the house. While old houses are notorious for drafts, we didn't feel any. We had to also consider the alternative, that old houses are also notorious for ghosts. Peter shut the door again with a firm shove, and we mutually agreed to move away from the door and sit in the exhibit room to the left of the entrance.

The incident was a valuable reminder that when conducting an investigation of a haunted site, it's best to "go in shooting"—ghostly activity does not always commence only after you have taken your sweet time setting up all of the cameras and equipment.

Still keeping one eye on the cellar door, Amy and I sat down for the interview. She asked some of the questions about which people are the most curious—how did I get into ghost hunting, what was the most bizarre haunting I had encountered, and where did I find the courage to crawl around in dark and dirty basements and attics, walk through cemeteries in the dead of night and come face to face with spirits from beyond the grave? While I responded in the most rational way possible, I was fully aware that rationality is a matter of opinion in such matters. Still, I always "call 'em as I see 'em." Or don't see them, as the case may be.

Mike Worden arrived and we finished up the interview while he set up his camera. Peter was first on camera with his historical background of Fort Decker and the surrounding area. I then spoke for a few minutes about my investigations and books. Bob later told me that during the time I was speaking, he had a funny feeling that we were not alone in the room and felt that he should take a photograph. The following is what came out.

Bob took this photo because he felt something strange at that moment.
An "orb" (center) appeared between Mike and I.

The orb in between Mike and I was the only such shape that appeared in any of the photographs taken that night. It is identical to other orbs that ghosts hunters have photographed at haunted locations around the world. There is a lot of controversy over what causes these orbs, and the explanations run the gamut from simple dust particles to a disembodied spirit in every orb. The most convincing piece of evidence here for me is the fact that Bob took this picture specifically because he felt a presence at *that* moment, and he in no way claims to be psychic or overly sensitive to such things. (Of course, I firmly believe that everyone has extrasensory abilities, it's simply a matter of paying attention and trying to develop them.)

When I sent this photo to Mike a few weeks later, he did some computer enhancing and saw that the light area above him seemed to take on the shape of a human form. While I am not always in favor of enhancing images or sound (don't get me started on that EVP!), there is some value to it if done properly and with some restraint. When enlarged and enhanced on the screen, that area does take on some human-like characteristics.

Obviously not knowing what had been captured on film, we proceeded to start the official "hunt," although, since I have no intentions of trying to "bag" a ghost, I prefer to call it an investigation. While Mike used his video camera, Bob used our camera in Nightshot mode, I carried the EMF meter and Amy had the non-contact thermometer. Peter led the way and we went first into the room across the hall, which originally had been the kitchen.

Almost immediately, the EMF meter showed high readings in the middle of the floor to the right of the fireplace. Peter pointed out the blackened ceiling beams overhead at that spot, the scars of a fire several generations ago. The house was supposed to be empty at the time of the fire and it is not believed that anyone was injured in the blaze. As he spoke, the high readings inexplicably faded away to nothing. It seemed that another cat and mouse game was on.

Moving over to the built-in corner shelf, the readings shot up again. Peter mentioned that this was the one piece that was original to the house. While it would have been fascinating if this old shelf was radiating over 200 years of collected energy, the readings appeared to be a little *too* high. Bob braved the cold to go out and examine the exterior of the structure in that area and reported that the electrical lines entered the house in this corner. Tending toward a natural electromagnetic field in this instance, it nonetheless did not explain the readings by the fireplace, which upon further examination came and went, and came again.

When we examined the infrared footage when we got home, we discovered (apart from the fact that in infrared I look like a blond with alien eyes!) that as I was standing on that spot explaining that something seemed to be going on, and asking if anyone was seeing anything, a strange white light darted in front of me and took off in the blink of an eye. Advancing the tape frame by frame, you can clearly see some object, no bigger than a quarter, enter from my left, pass in front of my hand, and then race off to my right.

My first inclination was to think that this was some kind of fly or some other winged insect, but then realized that the dead of winter is not exactly prime insect time, and the speed was greater than any insect I have ever seen. Also, during subsequent investigations at other locations, similar little, white (at least that's how it looks in infrared), fast-moving objects have darted through the field of view. Part of my routine is to be cognizant of any insect buzzing noises and to always be on the lookout for identifiable flying objects, but I have yet to be able to connect any insect life to these images. (I have purposely filmed bugs outside at night, and their speed and movement does not match this phenomena.)

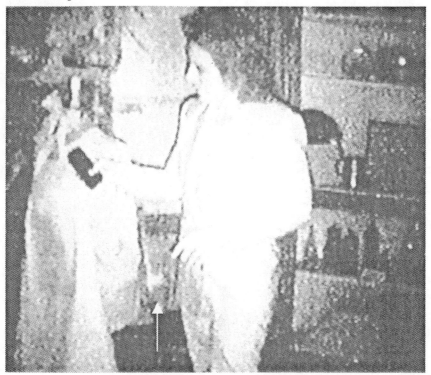

Here I am standing in the kitchen where the EMF meter was getting high readings. The arrow points to the light that appeared (in infrared) near my hand, moved to the left and then made a sharp right, all in the blink of an eye. The shelf to the right is the only original piece of furniture in the house. (By the way, I am wearing all black, but my clothing appears white in infrared.)

Once again, we did not know what we had captured on video at the time, and we proceeded on with the investigation. The basement was next, and I admit to being a little hesitant to pass through the door that had opened by itself. The basement was one of those typical dirt floor, stone wall cellars that lend themselves to tales of buried bodies. In fact, Peter told of a legend about a child who was accidentally killed and buried in the dirt of the cellar, but there was absolutely no evidence to substantiate any of those claims.

To my surprise, none of the equipment picked up anything unusual, and nobody's "internal sensors" felt anything, either. As creepy as it looked, it seemed "clean." After climbing the stairs back to the first floor, Peter

135

remarked that he was somewhat relieved that we did not come across anything, as some psychics in the past have practically run screaming from the basement. That's not to say that some terrifying entities do not inhabit that centuries-old cellar, but they did not make their presence known to us that night. Unless you count the door opening, of course.

There wasn't anything unusual on the upper floor, either, except in the room directly above the old kitchen. The corner that was over the built-in shelf had very high readings, which we once again attributed to the electrical lines. However, there was a return of the coming and going high readings in a spot in the middle of the floor, which exactly corresponded to the spot on the floor below where there were the high readings and the mysterious "flying spot." Peter could offer no explanation, nor could we find any natural reasons for this activity.

Returning to the exhibit room on the first floor, we discussed what had transpired, and what had not, which is often just as important. Peter showed us the photographs of past residents, and pointed out one in particular. It was a photo of a charming older woman, Mrs. Canfield, who had lived in the Fort Decker stone house for many years before it became a museum. Though somewhat reluctant to discuss her, as relatives still live in the area, he did relate a very important detail. A family member, hearing of the museum's bizarre light and alarm problem which generally occurred at the same hour, mentioned how this lady in her later years often went to bed about 9pm. However, regardless of the hour, Mrs. Canfield always followed the same routine before retiring—she would go from room to room and turn on the lights to make sure everything was secure.

Does Mrs. Canfield (seated, left) still make her rounds every night turning on the lights?

In the Spring of 2001, a nearby bridge was closed for repairs and local police were on duty to make sure traffic flowed smoothly. The policemen were positioned by the Fort Decker house and they all commented that they "watched the lights go on and off in the house all night." In fact, it happened with such frequency that after a while it no longer created any excitement.

Could this be a coincidence that many witnesses, including numerous police officers, have seen the lights go on? Does the former lady of the house still protect her

136

beloved home, following the same routine after death that she had so diligently followed in life?

And what of the opening door, the orb Bob captured on film in the exhibit room, or the strange readings and darting light in the old kitchen? Were these also pieces of evidence showing that the lady wants to make her presence known, or do other spirits from the house's turbulent 240 years of history also still cling to the site?

Visit Fort Decker, learn something about the history of the place and see what you feel. And don't worry if you get there after dark, someone will turn on a light for you.

LAUREL GROVE CEMETERY

Laurel Grove Cemetery is situated on a narrow peninsula between the Neversink and Delaware Rivers. The entrance to the cemetery is in Port Jervis, New York, but the opposite end has a tri-state marker that signifies it is the spot where New York, New Jersey and Pennsylvania converge. However, this cemetery may also be one spot where the world of the living converges with the world of the dead.

The cemetery received its first human remains in the mid-19th century. Over the generations, its ground was filled with both the wealthy and poor alike. Unfortunately though, as in life, the "haves and the have nots" do not share the ground equally. While the wealthy rest in peace beneath towering monuments on the flat sections in the center of the cemetery, the poor cling to the steep hillsides under dense overgrowth, many of who have no markers and are lost to history.

Such is the case with the old "colored section," which also contains the victim of one of the only lynchings in the Northeast. This was also the case with the nameless bodies that were swept from the riverbanks during a flood, going so far as Philadelphia before they were plucked from the water. No one knows how many corpses were washed away, or how many were never recovered.

Laurel Grove also contains the sad monument to a family who lost child after child at the tender ages of only a year or two. What joy it must have been when one daughter lived past her first and then second year. When she was approaching ten years of age, her parents must have believed that all of their prayers had been answered, until she was accidentally shot and killed by a hunter who mistook her for an animal as she played in the ruined foundation of an abandoned building.

There is also the recent grave of a woman who was murdered by her husband—on their wedding night. The tragedy is made all the more poignant when you see the simple marker surrounded by tributes to "Mom," left by her children from a previous marriage.

What other heart-wrenching tales lay hidden beneath the cold, gray stones? What sorrows are masked by the simple names and dates? A cemetery is indeed a place of great sadness, not only for the relatives and friends who come to grieve for their loved ones, but for the dead and buried who can not rest in peace because they were torn from this life too soon, or had too many regrets, or died with unfinished business. One can only wonder which of these reasons is behind the most frequently seen apparition of Laurel Grove—the woman in the gown.

She is not a new spirit; she has been seen for many generations. But as so often happens in such cases, the truth is blurred over time and a legend develops. These legends become part of local lore and while they make great campfire stories, eventually people cease to believe in them. And so it was with the lady of Laurel Grove, until she was seen again.

Several years ago, a boy died and was buried in the cemetery. His best friend was so distraught over his death that he left a note stating that he was going to commit suicide, and he was going to do it by his friend's fresh grave. The police were called and they rushed to the cemetery to try to prevent a second tragedy. As they searched the area, they saw a young woman in her early twenties wearing a long dress. They hoped she had seen the boy and so moved towards her. She moved away from them, but not by walking. The woman in the gown *floated* through the gravestones and disappeared. (The boy was found and did not commit suicide.)

In the last few years, other credible witnesses have reported seeing a figure drifting through the cemetery, only to vanish. Sometimes the apparition is distant and cannot be identified, but often one can clearly see the face and figure of woman, or catch a glimpse of a long dress fluttering behind the stones. Perhaps there are other ghosts who also walk the grounds, but what is the story behind this woman in the old-fashioned clothing? She appears to be so young—is she looking to recover those years that death stole from her? Or perhaps her corpse was one of those swept away and she searches for her eternal resting place in vain. Only she knows the answer, and so far she has yet to speak.

There are more tangible pieces of evidence of the restless dead in Laurel Grove. Occasionally, visitors make some rather grisly discoveries—bits of bone brought to the surface by burrowing ground hogs. Most recently someone found a human jawbone lying exposed near an animal den hole.

Unfortunately, not all of the exhumations are unintentional. Vandals have broken into mausoleums and exposed the corpses within. Whether this was done in an attempt to steal jewelry or was part of some black magic ritual is not currently known, as the twisted individuals have yet to be apprehended. As a result of these gruesome break-ins, all of the mausoleums have been bricked shut. However, this has not prevented other senseless acts of vandalism, such as knocking over monuments. Such actions may contribute to the spirits of the dead becoming restless.

Strange lights have also been photographed throughout the cemetery, seemingly hovering near certain gravestones. Aware of these inexplicable lights, as well as being aware that destructive vandals might be lurking about, a local policeman patrolling the cemetery recently called for backup when he spotted an eerily glowing light in the dead of night. The light did not move, and it burned brightly from a densely overgrown section about 40 feet from the road. When the other policemen arrived, they cautiously approached. What they discovered was a lighted mosquito trap attached to a tree by the health department!

This tall monument is in one of the areas where strange lights are seen.

In late June of 2001, Bob Strong and I arranged to meet Port Jervis Policeman Mike Worden and his girlfriend, Autumn Eherts, at Laurel Grove to do some investigating. It was a perfect summer's evening, and if you don't mind being surrounded by the dead, it is a beautiful setting nestled between the rivers. We grabbed our gear, piled into his Jeep and he proceeded to give us a tour.

About halfway through, we drove past three people who did not look as though they had come to pay their respects to the dead. A few feet further we caught the unmistakable scent of marijuana smoke. Turning the Jeep around, Mike flashed his badge and suggested they leave immediately, unless they preferred to get arrested. The three naturally protested their innocence, and one started to mouth off, but they all heeded the advice and left. Although the episode was brief and peaceful, it was nonetheless a strong reminder that I would rather face the spirits of the dead than deal with what police officers face every day in the line of duty.

Order restored, Mike drove us to a spot where a curious incident had occurred when he and another officer had stopped their patrol car one night. There was a loud tapping or knocking sound on the roof of their car, and they quickly rolled up the windows thinking it was some type of animal. Reaching for their flashlights, they got out of the car to take a look. The tapping sound stopped and there was no evidence that an animal had been on the car. Nor were they near any trees that could have been brushing against the car, and no branches or other objects were on the roof or ground. In short, there was no explanation for the sounds they both clearly heard.

Mike Worden stands in the area where the loud knocking sounds occurred on the roof of his patrol car. There are no trees above him, just open sky.

I scanned the area with the EMF meter, and there were a few brief seconds of moderately high readings near one of the taller monuments with a broken top, but nothing dramatic or conclusive. On the other side of the road was a mausoleum that had been vandalized a couple of years earlier and we decided to check that out next. In the grass to the left of the entrance, I saw a small, white object. Picking it up, I realized it was an angel figure. Bob took it and put it on the wall of the mausoleum and stepped back. He then began rubbing his hand across his forehead because he said it felt like a cobweb was lightly brushing across his skin. Although we had all just passed through that spot and felt nothing, and we were not under any tree, he continued to wipe his forehead several times, saying the feeling would not go away.

Then Mike, who was standing next to Bob, began getting the same sensation on his arm. He ran his hand down the length of his arm several times to wipe away whatever it was, but the sensation continued for about a minute. In the fading light I could see the hairs standing up on Mike's arm as if something was moving them. Then as suddenly as the feelings had come, both Bob and Mike reported they were gone.

This "cobweb" feeling they described was exactly what I had experienced at the Wershing home in New Jersey (see page 184). It is a most disturbing feeling, a tickling/tingling sensation as if something as light as a cobweb was running across your skin. Perhaps not by coincidence, I had also felt it on my forehead. Obviously, we all know what a real cobweb or spider web feels like, and we also know that once you brush it away the feeling stops. This sensation, however, does not stop when you try to brush it away, and the feeling also moves across your skin even if you are standing still.

Perhaps the tapping sounds and cobweb feelings by the vandalized mausoleum were the occupants' little reminders that they want to be left in peace. At that point, we were happy to oblige them.

Bob and Mike in the "cobweb zone."

Bats flying by the moon near the mausoleum provided great "atmosphere" for the ghost investigation.

We next went to examine an older section of the cemetery, which held the remains of several Civil War veterans. As we walked through the uneven rows, we came across a large hole dug by an animal. With some nervous laughter, we all commented that we hoped the light gray objects in the freshly dug dirt by the burrow entrance were just rocks. Bob gingerly picked up one of them, and fortunately it was indeed a rock, not a bony fragment of a corpse.

Dropping the rock and taking a step away, his foot came down on something hard. It was about a yard away from the hole and it was partially covered by the sandy soil that had been brought up by the industrious animals. Picking up the object and brushing it off, he was at first relieved to see that it was metal, not bone, but his relief was short-lived. Turning the piece of metal over in his hand, he recognized that it was an old, ornate casket handle!

Apparently, this rather heavy object was in the way of the animals' burrowing project and they must have expended considerable energy extracting it from their tunnel and dragging it to the surface. As the wooden grip of the handle had long since deteriorated, we assumed that the casket to which it had been affixed had also turned to dust, thereby exposing its human remains to both the elements and the clawing animals. The knowledge of what was going on right under our feet put very unsettling images in our minds, and we quickly placed the handle back where Bob found it and continued on. While you always try to expect the unexpected on a ghost hunt, this was one discovery for which none of us was prepared.

Bob holds the casket handle expelled from the hole by the new occupants of the gravesite.

It was starting to get late and we stopped by another mausoleum for a few final pictures. Feeling slightly uncomfortable, Autumn decided she did not want to get out of the Jeep. As soon as Mike, Bob and I climbed out, Bob once again got that "cobweb" sensation. I grabbed the camcorder from him and started shooting in Nightshot mode, but all I captured was him spinning in circles, vainly waving his hands in the air to push aside the phantom webs. Whatever it is, it certainly gets your attention.

Heading toward the exit of the cemetery, we caught sight of the mosquito light and understood how its eerie glow would have been cause for concern. We also saw other lights along the way—some were fireflies, and others were reflections off of the polished stones. There were also many strange sounds, but the geography of the place does lend itself to haunting echoes and distortions of distant voices. It would be difficult to walk among the dead of Laurel Grove at night and not feel something out of the ordinary, even if you knew nothing of the place.

However, if you go to Laurel Grove Cemetery aware of its tragic history, and knowing that the lady in the gown still drifts silently among the graves, while strange sensations play upon your skin and something knocks on your car while animals claw out nests underground amongst the corpses, you, too, may understand what it is like to not be able to rest in peace.

I took this photo near the tall monument just before we left because I had a strange sensation there—a pressure on my chest making it difficult to breathe. I told Bob about the feeling and how this area was "giving me the creeps" (not the most technical description, but accurate!). After I had the film developed, my blood ran cold when I saw what had been right in front of me. It is a black area with a white misty light inside of it. Notice the bottom of the light form is flat, as if part of it was in the ground, or rising up from it. Maybe it was a good thing that I didn't see this at the time!

A SAUCE TO DIE FOR

Italians are passionate about their food. To them, good cooking is both an art and a way of life. When a meal is prepared from an old family recipe, you can hear people exclaim, "This is just like Mama used to make!" Another common expression when tasting something delicious is that it is "to die for." In the case of this haunting, the food was actually something Papa made, and he literally did die for it.

In 1905, Rosario Prizzia knew that his family's tomato sauce recipe was too good to use only on the pasta on his table. Taking on a partner, the sauce entrepreneurs set up shop in a two-story stone building on Weeds Mill Road in Highland, New York. The sauce was prepared in huge cooking pots in quantities sufficient to feed the consumers hungry for this authentic Italian preparation. Tomatoes rolled into the factory from farms across the Hudson Valley, the sauce was carefully seasoned and cooked and the finished product was shipped out to the markets.

Business was good, the tomato sauce factory survived the early years of getting started and it looked as though it would last for generations. However, there were a couple of things the partners could not anticipate. For one, the advent of World War I in 1914 would mean boom times for American manufacturers of Italian food, as a German blockade effectively cut imports of tomato products. Another thing that the partners could not foresee was a tragic accident.

In 1913, just a year before profits might have skyrocketed, Mr. Prizzia died in a "bizarre explosion" at the factory. At that time, steam power was used and the boilers and machinery were notoriously unsafe. He was horribly burned in the explosion, never regained consciousness and was finally pronounced dead two days later. His partner was burned over 95% of his body, but managed to pull through.

By 1916, the surviving partner had taken the recipe and headed west to California where tomatoes grew plump and ripe, and where there was no danger of the killing frosts of the Northeast. In 1918, his new tomato sauce business took the name

Tony Prizzia and family still make kettles of sauce over wood fires.

Contadina (meaning "Woman of the Fields") and over eighty years later it is one of the most recognized names of tomato products in America.

Mr. Prizzia's name is not so well known. Although his descendants continue making the sauce with the original 1905 recipe, they now do it for Prizzia family tradition, not to manufacture it for the masses.

The factory building went on to be a speakeasy during Prohibition, and then a hotel. It is now an abandoned ruin, but it may not be as empty as it appears.

"Everyone in the neighborhood knew that place was haunted," said Jim Janso, who grew up just a few houses away from the old tomato sauce factory, and is now a policeman for the Town of Lloyd. "People used to see the figure of a man walking through the abandoned factory and standing by the second-story windows. We were terrified to even go near the place!"

While the stories of a ghostly figure of a man have been around for generations, it was only recently that Jim discovered there was some truth behind the stories of a terrible tragedy. Even more importantly, was the fact that it was a violent death, and both the date of the explosion and identity of the victim are known. Too frequently investigations of hauntings lead to nothing but legends and hearsay, so these were vital pieces of evidence.

When Rosario Prizzia's life was cut short so tragically, did his spirit fail to realize that his body had passed? Does he continue to walk the halls of the factory wondering why no one is there to cook the sauce, and does his spirit stand by the windows searching for his employees or the next delivery of tomatoes? Or perhaps there is some message he needs to deliver to the living, some personal words to his family or something regarding the business and his secret recipe. Or could it be, by some terrible circumstance, that his spirit is restless because the explosion could have been avoided, that some simple maintenance or the turning of a valve could have prevented his untimely death?

One can only speculate, but the facts remain that a man was killed because of that factory, and for many years after the place was empty and abandoned, yet a man could still be seen in that building.

"When I got older," Jim said, "I thought that maybe the ghost story was just one of those neighborhood legends made up to scare kids. Had I known that someone had actually died, I think I would have told my parents that we had to move!"

No doubt much to Jim's further dismay, in addition to the spirit of the man whose life ended so tragically within the old stone walls, there may be other shadows of the building's colorful past still clinging like the thick vines that enshroud it. Many people have reported that when entering the empty building they immediately hear a voice speaking softly. If they then had the courage to ascend the main staircase, there were other sounds to be heard—sounds of plates and glasses clinking, and music being played. As they climbed the stairs listening to these sounds, they fully expected to find a party in full swing on the second floor. What they would find would be nothing.

No glasses of champagne, no plates of hors d'oeuvres, no musicians and not a single living soul.

When the factory became a speakeasy in the 1920s, there must have been some wild parties as the illegal bootleg liquor flowed. (Tony Prizzia—Rosario's grandson—confirmed that there was an illegal still operation just down the road at the time.) Often, such places also provided gambling and prostitution—ingredients that when mixed with potent alcohol and the tough mobsters who ran the speakeasies, could create explosions of a different, but equally deadly kind. Had some awful crime or tragic event occurred at one of these parties, condemning those present to relive the scene over and over throughout eternity? Or do the souls of those who drank and danced and forgot their cares for a few hours still return every night to try to recapture some small measure of the happiness they knew there?

***

In June of 2001, Jim Janso corresponded with me by e-mail about my ghost stories, inquiring as to when I might be coming out with a new book. I told him a new one was in progress and if he knew of any haunted locations to let me know as I was still collecting material. He then mentioned a "haunted tomato factory," and while there weren't many details, my curiosity was definitely peaked. Ghost investigations can lead you to some bizarre locations, but I never thought a tomato sauce factory would be on that list!

I asked what night we could go to the factory and take a look. Old childhood fears are not easy to discount, however, and at first Jim flatly refused to go, especially at night. He explained that even though his police work has brought him into life-threatening situations, and he has witnessed horrible fatal accidents, the prospect of going to this factory was more than he could handle.

This was an amusing reminder to me that the things I do and the places I go in the course of my investigations are not exactly normal, to put it mildly. Perhaps fools do rush in where angels fear to tread, but I am far more concerned about the living who may be lurking in abandoned buildings and cemeteries. I made the lighthearted suggestion that if he could protect me from the living, I would try to protect him from the dead. Summoning his courage, Jim agreed.

On a beautiful Saturday afternoon in July 2001, Bob and I met Jim at a commuter parking lot at the intersection of Routes 9W and 299. We followed him a mile or so to a quiet residential street. After going a few blocks from the main road, Jim put on his left turn signal by an overgrown field and we wondered where he was planning on taking us.

Turning onto the knee-high grass, we followed, and fortunately came to a stop at the edge of the shoulder-high grass. We got out of the van, looked at the dense growth of trees and vines in front of us and just put it on faith that Jim knew where he was going. Grabbing the bags of equipment, I asked how

146

far back we would have to hike. Jim pointed to the tangle of green not fifty feet ahead and said that was the factory!

Looking more closely, hints of stone could be seen amidst the vines, and the wall of vegetation did appear to be just that, almost flat like a wall. I don't know exactly what I had expected, but this was clearly the most dilapidated site I had ever visited. We walked through the tall grass around the back to the "main entrance," which was essentially the only door you could get to without using a machete. The ancient-looking stone walls towering above us did indeed seem to have many stories to tell, and the history of the place felt as thick as the vegetation that clung to its craggy surface.

Jim Janso and Bob Strong, standing just a
few yards away from the overgrown factory walls.

Jim pushed open the door about eighteen inches, which was as far as it would go. He then moved a precariously balanced beam off to the side as Bob cautioned me to keep an eye on the bricks tenuously mortared over the doorway. Unfortunately, a hard hat and body armor were not on our equipment roster.

Sidestepping carefully through the narrow opening, the derelict factory finally presented itself in its full state of deterioration. The roof was completely collapsed, the weight of which had also brought down most of the second floor. I wondered if Mr. Prizzia's spirit was also brought down to the ground level by the collapse.

The staircase directly in front of us looked like something out of a funhouse, with its first few steps completely missing. Leaving everything by the door except for a couple of cameras, we crawled under the staircase and stepped our way over and under beams and debris to the left where the floor above our heads was still intact. An old piano stood rotting off to the side, rusted chairs scattered the floor and the musty odor of decay hung heavily in the air. It was very quiet and still, but I was cognizant of the fact that a deafening explosion had once rocked these walls, taking a man's life.

Jim said there was a cooler in the back corner and he wasn't too anxious to look inside. Bob handed me a flashlight across the crumbling piano keyboard and I picked my way back to the spot Jim indicated. What I had thought was a small icebox was in reality a full walk-in refrigerator or freezer. Shining the light inside, I was amazed at the pristine condition of the wood; the inside of the roughly ten-foot square refrigerator looked almost brand new. I started to step inside, but the floor was bending beneath my foot and I didn't relish the thought of plunging into some ancient basement (or worse). I also didn't care for the sight of the rows of sharp meat hooks running along the back wall and decided a picture taken in the doorway was good enough.

The remains of the staircase which went to the second floor where Mr. Prizzia's spirit was seen walking, and where the sounds of a party could often be heard.

Leaving that section, we worked our way through the maze of fallen beams to the other side of the old factory. Here the roof and second floor had come crashing down and the scene presented itself as more of a dangerous house of cards. A misplaced hand or foot could easily bring down enough debris to allow the tomato factory to claim at least a second victim. As we paused to look around, there was a noise that came from the second floor area, as if something had been dropped. We all heard it, but with birds and animals having full access, the sound could easily have been made by a living creature. Of course, under the circumstances, it was possible it hadn't been made by anything living.

We poked gingerly in the debris, hoping to find something with a name or date, or anything to provide some clues to the place. There were scraps of wallpaper painted to look like drapery on the few remaining sections of wall. There were railings from a staircase that no longer existed, an old woman's shoe, some broken plates and cups—all stark reminders that nothing in this life is permanent.

I took some photographs, Bob took one of me near a brick supporting column, and then we decided that we had seen enough. As we were packing up to leave, I realized that I hadn't even taken the thermometer or EMF meter out their case. Deciding that since I had crawled through the place once already, it wouldn't hurt to go through a second time and see if there were any unusual readings. While Bob and Jim stood by the front entrance, I went back through the factory alone, checking for any cold spots or electromagnetic fields.

The left side of the building, which was a bit creepier because of the darkness (and the meat locker!), had no fluctuations in temperature and the EMF meter held steady around zero. In a place that had no computers, refrigerators, electrical appliances or any electricity at all, there wasn't anything to generate electromagnetic fields and give misleading readings. If the meter indicated any readings, they would clearly be some of the most inexplicable ones I would ever get.

When I made my way back behind the staircase near the front door, I was tempted to just say the heck with the rest of the building and leave, as the rotting stench and dangerous conditions were having an effect, but I snapped out of it and continued on to the right side. As I carefully chose where to put down each foot, my eye caught a quick spike on the EMF meter. Not sure if I had actually seen what I thought I just saw, I backed up half a step and the meter went back up.

"Uhhh, guys, I think I have something here," I shouted to Bob and Jim who had been chatting as they waited for my return. There was a second of silence and then they asked what I had found. I told them I had detected an electromagnetic field in one spot. I then realized that it was the exact spot where I had been standing when we heard the noise, and it also just happened to be the spot where Bob had decided to take my picture.

I am standing on the spot where there was an inexplicable electromagnetic field. The collapsed second floor is on the left.

They both worked their way back over to where I stood, and we scraped at the debris at our feet to see if there was any reason for a field to be present. Under the decaying wood doors and beams we found only a solid concrete floor. I handed the meter to Bob and moving it slowly from side to side, he confirmed that in a narrow region, roughly ten inches wide and from the floor to a height of a little over five feet, there was indeed a definite and inexplicable electromagnetic field.

At this point we seemed to be faced with three possibilities. 1) The meter was malfunctioning, although it was only doing so on this one spot. 2) There was some natural underground source of the field that reached up through the concrete floor in just a short, narrow area. 3) We were standing face to "face" with Rosario Prizzia, or some other disembodied spirit who didn't mind making its presence known in the broad daylight of a warm and sunny summer's day. I was suddenly glad I hadn't come here in the dark.

As always, I tried to remain objective about what I saw, but that little trickle of fear was nonetheless creeping up my spine. Although rushing out was surely an option, we calmly crawled our way back to the doorway, squeezed our way outside and all took a long, deep breath.

If there are spirits in the ruins of the old factory building, how long will they still cling to the rotting beams and decaying walls? Even if the building is completely leveled and a new structure is built on the site, is there any guarantee that the ghosts will not take their place in the new residence? If that does ever happen, hopefully the new owners will know how to make a tomato sauce that is to die for...

Early 1900s photo of the man killed in the factory explosion,
Rosario Prizzia (far right), in his bar in New York City.
Photo courtesy of Anthony Prizzia (Rosario's great-grandson.).
Photo restored by Aaron Weed, PC Solutions.

COMPASSION AND GRATITUDE

Town of Lloyd policeman Jim Janso has seen worse things than the spirits of the dead. He has seen the pain and suffering of the dying.

While policeman, firemen and EMS workers witness the aftermath of automobile accidents on a daily basis, there are some that are so horrific the memory will never leave those who were on the scene. And if one of the victims of an accident happens to come back from the dead and visit you in your bedroom, that would make it an even more memorable event.

At 8:50 am on a Monday in May of 1999, a woman driving on Route 299 (in NY) slowed down to make a left turn in the eastbound lane. Moments later, a tractor trailer filled with powdered cement rammed into the back of her station wagon, sending her and her 4-year-old child across the westbound lane and into the woods. Fortunately, both mother and child were wearing seatbelts and did not sustain any serious injuries.

The driver of the cement truck was not so lucky. As his tractor trailer veered onto the shoulder after the impact, he overcorrected and swung into the westbound lane, directly into the path of another tractor trailer filled with paper. The two heavy, massive vehicles collided head-on. The explosive impact could be heard over a mile away and debris and twisted wreckage was scattered for a quarter of a mile. Newspaper accounts echo the same words from all of the witnesses—it was the worst accident they had ever seen.

The remains of one of the trucks. Photo courtesy of Jim Janso

When Officer Janso arrived he felt like he was walking into a war zone. His first thought was that the scene looked like the Iraqi convoy that was obliterated as it tried to flee Kuwait during the Gulf War. Axles, engine parts,

151

metal and glass were everywhere. The man who had been driving the truck filled with paper had been killed instantly. The cab of the cement truck was crushed and upside down, so Jim assumed that the driver of that vehicle had also died on impact. However, as he walked past, he heard a strange moaning sound.

That driver was alive, although barely, and he was pinned underneath the cab. He had not been wearing his seatbelt and the terrible crash had thrown him from the cab, which then came to rest on top of him. Not knowing whether or not the man was conscious and could understand him, Jim assured him he was going to get help.

An auto mechanic's garage was just a short distance down the road and Jim rushed to the garage to get a heavy-duty jack. Several people then used the jack to raise the smashed cab while Jim and a couple of EMS workers pulled the man free from the wreckage. It was painfully obvious that this accident was about to claim the life of a second victim. Even though it was clear there was no hope, and even though the man appeared incapable of understanding what was being said, Jim stayed by his side and kept speaking words of encouragement.

The two drivers were transported to local hospitals where they were both pronounced dead on arrival. Route 299 was closed for eight hours while spilled fuel and wreckage was removed. As night fell, there was no longer any indication that a fatal accident had occurred on that spot, and it would quickly fade from the memory of local residents.

Jim Janso was terribly shaken by what he had seen that day—the twisted metal, the mangled flesh, the shattered lives. These images would never leave his memory. That night he tried to sleep, but he tossed and turned as the scene continued to replay in his mind. In the middle of the night, he turned yet again to look at the clock on the nightstand. What he saw by his bed was something else he would never forget.

Standing just a few feet away was the man he had helped pull from the wreckage, the man he had continued to speak to when words had seemed useless. But he did not appear as a bloody figure in shredded clothes. The deceased driver was wearing the same flannel shirt, blue jeans and work boots in which he had died, but they were now clean and undamaged.

Officer Jim Janso

The man also appeared healthy and unharmed. As Jim stared in silent amazement, the man simply smiled and said, "Thank you." Then he vanished.

While a dead man by his bed was an even a greater shock than the accident scene, in the following days Jim was able to gain some comfort from the driver's apparition. Although the man had been through a terrible ordeal, the manner of his appearance seemed to indicate that he was all right now. And the fact that the driver had come back to thank Jim meant that his efforts had not been in vain, that he had been able to provide comfort to someone in his last moments of life.

At the time, he didn't tell many people about his unearthly visitor, because he knew he would get kidded about it, and that everyone would think he was just dreaming or imagining it. Jim Janso knows he was wide awake. He knows that the spirit of the driver crossed one more road to show his gratitude.

THE HOSPITAL ROOMMATE

If a spirit tends to linger where the body drew it last breath, then surely hospitals must be among the most haunted places on Earth. As much as they are places in which to bring new life into the world and heal the sick of all ages, they are also places of death, places where grieving family members and friends undergo the terrible ordeal of losing a loved one.

Several doctors, nurses and staff members have told me that the general public has no idea of the strange things that go on in hospitals. They whisper a few tantalizing suggestions, imply that there are terrifying tales to be told, and then refuse to give any details for fear of losing their positions. To date, not a single health care professional has had the courage to come forward to say just what does go bump in the night in your local hospital. Finally in March of 2001, however, a patient in a New Jersey hospital came forward—a man who just might have faced death in more ways than one.

Gary was forty-five and successfully running the business he had inherited from his father. Then a sudden life-threatening illness brought him to the hospital in November of 1999. The story is best told in his own words:

"Aside from learning the hard way that a rare disease isn't just a convention of the soap operas, and what intensive care was like, I got my own scary story out of the deal...as if I wasn't scared enough at the time.

I'd gone off intensive care and had been sharing a room with another guy. He got better and went home, so I had the room to myself for a couple days. I wasn't unhappy about this, as this guy ran the TV set 24 hours a day, and every minute of it talk shows. However, that night it seemed like I was sharing my room with...someone.

I woke up late at night to hear somebody coughing loudly, a real uncontrollable fit. I turned over to see if I had to summon the nurse, in case my roommate was having a choking fit. However, seeing the empty bed (even in the dark I could see the bed) reminded me that he was out, and nobody else had moved in with me yet. The coughing went on for about ten minutes. Now I can be calm about it. At the time, though, what I thought was: 'Oh God, there's a ghost in the room with me, and he's still sick!'

No, I didn't dare ask the nurses later if there was any talk of a haunted room. I was too grateful that the coughing only happened once, and also too beholden to the hospital for saving my life to quibble about a little thing like a ghost in my room."

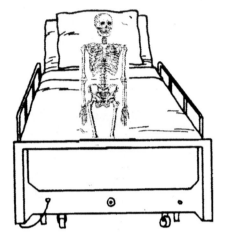

As time passed in the hospital, Gary came to believe that the invisible choking man in the next bed was merely a trick of the acoustics, coupled with the strain of his illness and the medication he was being given. However, he now concedes that, "I might have just convinced myself of the acoustic story to keep from worrying."

After asking him a series of questions, the picture became a little clearer. For starters, he was indeed on several medications, although this was the only incident he experienced during the almost four weeks he was in the hospital. If the drugs in his system could cause hallucinations, one would expect there to be numerous such incidences. He did, however, have several vivid nightmares during his stay. The worst occurred within his first few days when he dreamed that his bed "was surrounded by a crowd of grim, threatening people."

Perhaps it was the stress, the illness or the drugs. Or, just possibly, his unconscious mind could perceive the lost souls that wander the halls and look for seriously ill patients who might soon be joining them.

Also, Gary was definitely awake during the phantom coughing episode and clearly felt the presence of someone else in the room, even though no one could be seen. And the position of the beds in the room would tend to discount the acoustic trick theory.

The door to the room was open, and Gary occupied the bed closest to the open door, yet the sound was clearly coming from the other bed. If someone down the hall was having a coughing fit, why couldn't he hear the sound coming through the door? How could this terrible sound bounce silently around corners and manifest itself in the exact spot where a real person would have been? And if someone was indeed choking to death, why didn't any nurses, staff or other patients respond in the lengthy span of at least ten minutes?

Perhaps the answer is that this particular patient was already dead, and only Gary had the ability to hear his tormented coughing. But was this just a single occurrence from a patient who had just recently died in that room, or was it the sickly soul of a man who had passed years ago and is still trying to let his roommates know he needs help?

Time and time again, I am asked why hauntings of this nature (or any, for that matter) occur. Unfortunately, few people are lucky enough to pass on when they are good and ready. All too often they die too suddenly, with too much unfinished business and too many words not spoken. While it is comforting to think that all of our troubles melt blissfully away once we "walk into the light," the concept is about as realistic as jumping out of a plane with an umbrella and thinking you will make a soft landing. The real trick is to unload as much of your baggage as you can during life, so you don't hit so hard once you land on the other side. Take care of your health, take care of your problems and always be cognizant of the fact that it really isn't over when it's over!

As Gary theorized after his brush with death: "...the people there have all the vices and foibles that they used to make themselves and other people miserable during their lifetimes, and they are just as blind to their faults now as they were then. And perhaps they hold on to more than their faults, perhaps they might also bring the illnesses and insanities that made their life horrible over here onto the other side as well..."

NO MORE ROOM AT THE INN

After giving a ghost talk to a teen reading group at the Goshen library in October 2000, I was contacted by library employee Linda Pederson. She was acquainted with the owner of the Orange Inn, which is just a few doors down on the next block, and indicated that the Inn might have some very old residents—as much as 200 years old.

We arranged to meet with Mimi LaBurt, the owner, on the evening of December 4. We sat in the bar/dining area and while Mimi was getting something for us to drink (non-alcoholic, I should point out!), I switched on the EMF meter and found that I was already getting high readings. When Mimi returned she explained that a lot of the sightings have taken place in the bar area, which is part of the structure built in 1790. Over the years numerous people have seen men dressed in what is described to be "Abe Lincoln clothing." There have also been reports of a woman in a blue nightgown, as well as dark shadows and forms that do not reveal their identity.

None of the spirits in the bar area are malevolent, but Mimi said she does get the feeling they like to play games with her on occasion. That is not surprising as I have seen such mischievous activity on several investigations and have concluded that for some reason death increases one's proclivity for practical jokes.

Gathering up the equipment, we began with the hallway leading to the kitchen. Readings became even higher and peaked outside the Ladies Room door. And lo and behold, the readings went up and down and up again in the same spot, almost as if something was playing games with us. Mimi said that several people have reported an icy cold feeling in the Ladies Room, as well as a feeling of someone else being there. Psychics have described that hallway as a type of passageway between the world of the living and the dead. We would encounter someone entering that passageway on our next visit, although that night we already knew this was not an ordinary hallway.

Continuing into the kitchen, Mimi recalled that soon after opening the restaurant, she and chef Jim Hall were sitting in the kitchen discussing business. Suddenly a large pan came off a shelf and flew through the air directly at them, almost hitting Jim. So much for the welcoming committee. Jim has often seen dark figures in the kitchen, although thankfully no more cookware has been hurled at him.

The dining room is a lovely area with a colonial theme and windows all along the front. The EMF meter immediately began to go a bit crazy in the dining room, and after a considerable effort to pinpoint where the readings were coming from I found that they seemed to be near wherever Linda P. was standing. I asked her if she was feeling anything unusual and she said her feet were warm and tingling (not something that usually happens) and she was a little lightheaded. I asked Bob to take a photo (right) and what came out was a streak of light that appeared to be over Linda P. (I have been back to see if perhaps a ceiling light or any reflection could have caused this effect, but there was no tangible explanation.)

Our next stop was the front desk, which by the way, is no ordinary desk. It was once owned by George M. Cohan (if you never heard of him, go rent "Yankee Doodle Dandy" starring James Cagney), who was a relative of Mimi's family. History lesson aside, there was an interesting story behind the desk.

One night one of the bartenders, Rick, sat down at the desk to call his girlfriend. It was late and no one else was around, but suddenly a female voice yelled, "Get out of *my* chair!" He didn't need to be told twice. Rick also complained about dark figures around the bar and strange things going on. Rick doesn't work at the Orange Inn any longer.

After a little more exploring on the first floor, it was time for the basement. Although the Inn was built in 1790, the basement is much older. Originally, the courthouse stood on this site and its basement was the prison. Such infamous characters as Claudius Smith, the outlaw "Cowboy of the Ramapos," was confined there before he was taken out into the square and hung. When the old courthouse was razed, the prison basement remained and the inn was built on top of it. Perhaps the Inn "inherited" some of those unhappy souls who spent their last hours in those cells?

As we entered the basement, Mimi warned us that it was a bit confining (no pun intended) in portions of the "dungeon," as she jokingly referred to it. When we saw the tunnel-like passage we would have to practically crawl through, we realized it was no joke.

Bob carried the cameras while I had the EMF meter and thermometer. Once we squeezed through the narrow passage, the area opened into the old prison section. At one point I heard what sounded like a child sighing, but no one else heard it so I chalked it up to creaking floorboards overhead. Later, Mimi's uncle Gino asked if we had heard any of the ghosts of the children in the basement. I began to rethink the floorboard hypothesis.

There was one spot in the old prison section that seemed colder and had high EMF readings. I asked Mimi if there was any significance to that spot and she said that one psychic sensed the spirit of a man who was imprisoned there. I asked Bob to take a few more photos as Mimi, Linda P. and I headed back through the passageway. Linda P. was behind me,

One of the narrow passageways in the "dungeon."

and halfway through I heard a loud *bang* against one of the pipes just inches from my head. I thought Linda P. had slipped and struck her head against one of the heavy pipes so I spun around to see if she was okay. She was fine— she hadn't slipped or even touched the pipes.

"Then what was that banging noise?" I asked, an instant before a second banging sound rang along the pipes, then a third and fourth...

157

There we were in a dark, dirty, spider web-infested dungeon tunnel and something was slamming against those old pipes as if they were being smashed with a heavy wrench.

"Mimi, do these pipes ever make noise?" I asked, suddenly feeling a bit trapped.

"No, I never heard them do that!" she responded with some concern. "I sure hope we aren't getting them mad at us!"

We hurried out of the tunnel and back into the renovated section of the basement where we could at least stand up straight. I was about to take a deep breath in relief, but the air stopped in my throat as I stood up and looked right into a white, misty cloud about ten feet in front of me. It was several feet wide and stretched from the ceiling to about a foot above the floor.

Mimi and Linda P. were right behind me and I asked, "Mimi, do you ever see anything like *that* down here?"

"No, I have never seen anything like *that!*" she replied. "I think I want to get the hell out of here, now!"

My initial reaction was also to leave, but in moments like this I find I'm usually far more curious and stubborn than scared, although it was close. I reached for a camera, but realized that Bob had all of the camera equipment on the other side of the tunnel. I shouted for him to hurry back and come out shooting.

Inching a little closer, I saw that the mist was swirling and undulating, yet remaining in the same spot by a pillar. Seconds seemed like hours as I waited for Bob and the cameras, and the mist began to fade. Fearing it would disappear more than I feared it, I stepped forward and thrust my hand right into it. This white cloud was cool, but not cold, and it felt denser, heavier than the surrounding air. As the last wisps swirled across my hand, Bob emerged, camera ready, but it was too late. He saw it for a second, but in the instant it took to raise the camera and take the picture it had vanished.

The four of us stood there for a minute agreeing that we all saw it, but we didn't know what it was we saw. Still trying to remain practical and examine every possibility, I checked the temperature of the nearby pipes to see if steam had caused the knocking or the mist, but the pipes were cold to the touch— 59 degrees, to be exact. And the mist into which I had thrust my hand definitely did not feel like hot steam. It was one of the most remarkable things we had ever witnessed on a ghost investigation.

Unfortunately, we didn't capture it on film, which still galls me to this day. It was a painful, yet valuable, reminder not to put all your cameras in one basket. If an investigation team is going to split up, at least one member in every group needs a camera. As I've said before, ghosts generally don't sit around waiting for you to get your act together.

Still, we had four witnesses to the swirling mist, and that, combined with the knocking sounds, child's sigh and high EMF readings, added up to a rather successful evening. However, the evening was still young.

We continued on with the upper floors and the other half of the Inn. I had no idea it was so big, with so many rooms, hallways and staircases. Many of the rooms were occupied by tenants, so Mimi let us into the few that were vacant. In one room there were some high EMF readings on the bed, and nowhere else. An elderly woman had lived in that room for many years and had passed away recently. I would bet she still hadn't checked out completely yet.

As Mimi opened another large, dark room, I pointed the thermometer inside, looking for cold spots and got a reading of 80 degrees. I laughed, thinking that I had aimed it directly at the radiator. Mimi was concerned, however, and said that there was no way the radiator should be up so high in a vacant room. She flicked on the light and walked into the room, turning left. This was confusing, because I hadn't pointed the thermometer in that direction.

Stepping inside, I saw that the radiator was indeed off to the left, and it was just as cold as the rest of the room. The spot where I had gotten the temperature of 80 degrees was a bare section of wall directly under the window. It was a cold day, the window was cold, the radiator was cold and nothing in the room was generating any kind of heat.

Bob videotaped the entire incident and there I am standing there saying, "I've run into plenty of cold spots, but never a warm spot!" In fact, I am so puzzled I say it twice. Unless there is some type of heater running, the only time I would get a reading of 80 degrees in a situation like that is if I point the thermometer at a living human being. The one thing I can guarantee is that there

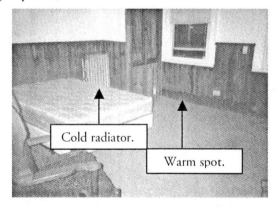

Cold radiator.

Warm spot.

were no living beings in that room when Mimi first opened the door. The "warm spot" has become yet another mystery of the Orange Inn.

Mimi's apartment was also interesting. I felt very uncomfortable in there. Mimi has seen the figure of a woman walk across the floor and vanish. A psychic told her that there was a dark, negative energy in those rooms. This was the same psychic who sensed the imprisoned man in the dungeon and she became completely unnerved by what she experienced at the Inn. She also claimed some of the Inn's spirits followed her home. She was supposed to return for further investigation. She never did.

And just when we thought it was safe to descend the stairs of the Orange Inn, we discovered there was a second basement. While it did not contain any of the original foundation or dungeon, it was nonetheless "creepy," as Linda P. so aptly put it. There was a lonely, almost desperate feeling to the place. When Bob started shooting video in the Nightshot mode, he almost immediately reported some white spots of light darting by. We could not see them, but the infrared camera captured several in that area. Our 35mm photos later revealed a white, hazy cloud in that same section. By this point, I had come to the inescapable conclusion that there was never a dull moment, or an empty room, at the Orange Inn.

The darting light taped in infrared.

Mimi said that many years earlier an old tombstone was found in the basement. It had once marked the grave of a woman who had lived in Goshen about 200 years ago, but how it ended up in that basement was another mystery. Had this woman been buried in the basement for some strange reason? Had she been buried on that spot earlier, and her grave wasn't discovered until the building was underway? Had her body been moved to the basement after being buried somewhere else? Or, had someone simply taken the grave marker and hidden it in the basement?

Whatever the case, perhaps it is her spirit in the basement, either lingering where her body was buried, or looking for the tombstone that should be above her eternal resting place.

We all needed our own rest after the investigation. Not only did it feel like we had walked miles through the labyrinth of corridors, rooms and basements, there is a certain high intensity level that comes with not knowing what is going to jump out at you from one second to the next. As we powered down the equipment, and ourselves, we nonetheless talked about coming back. I told Mike Worden all

This photo was taken in the "newer" section of the basement and a white haze appears along the right side.

160

about our adventures, and he was very anxious to tape another show at the Inn.

We let the hectic holiday season pass and planned to meet one Saturday afternoon in January. I spent a couple of hours checking camera and tape recorder batteries, film, flashlights, etc.—the usual "pre-flight" routine. I was more excited about our return trip to the Orange Inn since now I knew how active the place really was. Bob and I met Linda P., Mike and Autumn in the lobby, but due to some mix-up in communications Mimi never arrived. All geared up and no ghosts to hunt! As part of my routine involves getting mentally psyched (essentially convincing myself that whatever the spirit world can dish out, I can take), it's tough to just walk away and unwind. However, I'm sure I found some way to dispel the pent-up energy.

We rescheduled for February 10, and although business prevented Mimi from being with us again, she left instructions that we should feel free to go wherever we wanted. Retracing our steps from the first visit, we found many of the same readings. We also found some things we didn't expect.

As we were all standing in the hall by the Ladies Room, Mike began to feel an icy cold mass of air around him. We all confirmed that exactly where Mike was standing it felt about 30 degrees cooler. The EMF readings were also high. We all checked the length of the hallway to see if there were any drafts, but all the doors were closed and there weren't any vents. And the only place it felt cold was around Mike.

As Bob was filming the four of us standing there with our hands reaching into the cold area, we heard a banging sound coming from the kitchen, approximately 25-30 feet from where we were standing. We all looked up toward the door and I asked, "What was that?"

Before anyone could reply, the kitchen door slowly creaked open by itself! I suppose I had better mention that we were the only ones in this part of the building—no living soul was in that kitchen! If this was a psychic passageway, we all had just witnessed a spirit opening the door and walking in. Fortunately, we had learned from our white mist (or should I say missed) episode in the basement on our last visit and this time Bob was there with the camera rolling and got the entire thing on video.

After a stunned pause, I went down the hall and closed the door again. The door kind of sticks into place and it does take a considerable shove to open it. There isn't any rational explanation as to why that door would open by itself. I have to admit I was very pleased that we had witnessed and taped such an exciting event, but there was more to come that day.

Unfortunately, the newer section of basement was locked, but the old dungeon section was open. We crawled around once again, explaining for Mike's show what had occurred on the previous investigation. Bob was also filming and while none of us heard anything unusual at the time, as he was passing by the area where the pipes had started banging the last time, there

We all turn and watch the kitchen door open by itself.
(Infrared image.)

was a brief childlike laugh or giggle caught on tape. It is very clear, and very unusual, and no one recalls actually hearing anything like it at the time. Was this one of the spirits of the little children letting us know that they were responsible for the pipe "prank"?

When we were finished taping for Mike's show, I suggested we just sit quietly in the dungeon for a few minutes with the lights off. As you are walking around with meters and cameras, trying not to whack your head on a beam or twist an ankle, you are concentrating on a different type of activity. I thought by just sitting and listening, we might pick up something on a different level.

I picked a spot on the floor where I had first seen the white mist and sat down to wait. I didn't have to wait long. Within a minute, very cold air rushed in around me. I slipped the thermometer out of my pocket and took an instant reading—48 degrees. It had been 61 degrees when I sat down. This thermometer gives a constant digital reading and I watched as the cold air moved off and the temperature jumped back to 61 degrees. Just to make sure "it" had my attention, the cold air moved over me again, the temperature dropped to 48 degrees, lingered for perhaps 15 or 20 seconds and was gone. I would say my little experiment worked.

During the summer of 2001, as I was writing *Haunted Hudson Valley 3*, I got the following e-mail from Linda Pederson:

"A strange story for you:

On a Saturday morning about two weeks ago I went over to the Orange Inn and went in the old jail part of the basement and stayed down there for about 45 minutes by myself. Nothing out of the ordinary happened which was a little disappointing. However, when I decided to go back upstairs to the dinning room near the bar THE DOOR WAS LOCKED!

I knocked on the door several different times and waited for someone to come. When no one came I tried to get out the back door that was held shut with the handle of a pair of pliers running through a loop through which you would put a padlock. I took the pliers out and pulled hard on the door and guess what, I COULD NOT GET OUT!

At this point I was becoming a little concerned. I then used the pliers to bang on the door to the dinning area and waited a while longer. It was then that I was hit with a sudden feeling of "I don't want to die here," which was very strange since I had not been overly anxious about my situation until that point. I put my hand above my head and could feel very warm air just in the upper space of the basement.

While using my hand to test the temperature of the air above me I noticed the brick wall that is there and saw the pattern of what looked like an archway. I think you may have noticed it when we went there together, I'm not sure though.

It was not long after this that Mimi came and let me out. She had been in the large dinning area setting up for a party of some sort when she thought she heard a noise, that's when she realized that she had not seen me come back up from the basement and went to check.

She said that I could have gotten out the back door since that was not locked. I told her that I had tried. She then went to the back door and was able to open it. She then asked me if I would like to sit down for a while and have a drink to get the cobwebs out. I thanked her but declined since I had other errands to run."

If there are those who doubt the existence of ghosts, I would say the old dungeon basement of the Orange Inn could cure them of their skepticism. The spirits of the condemned prisoners and the little children appear more than willing to prove that death is just another step, not a finality.

Or perhaps these skeptics would like to feel the chill of the hallway and watch doors open by themselves, or sit in the bar area and wait for the lady in the blue nightgown. And let's not forget the darting orbs of light, the white, misty cloud, the children's laughter, the mysterious electromagnetic fields and the inexplicable warm spot.

163

For hundreds of years, the Orange Inn has seen thousands of people come and go. Why, then, would it be so difficult to believe that a few have decided to stay?

***

Just when I thought our bizarre experiences at the Orange Inn were over, I saw this photo when my film was developed. On the evening of December 4, after our investigation, I decided to take a few pictures of the outside of the building. All of the pictures came out normal, except this one.

I always say that if I can't get an absolutely undeniable photo of a ghostly figure, I would rather get no image at all. Unfortunately, while this isn't an indisputable phantom photo, it certainly looks like a transparent human figure standing right in front of me, from the middle of the chest up. (The original color photo is much clearer and more well defined.) This strange effect was not in any of the other pictures and I half wish it wasn't in this one.

I don't run around claiming that every spot of light in a photograph is a ghost, and I make no claims on this one. As always, I simply present it to you and let you draw your own conclusions.

MAN (AND WOMAN'S) BEST FRIEND

I don't think I have ever referred to my dogs as pets. They are my friends, a part of my family. Anyone who has ever been fortunate enough to form an emotional bond with an animal knows that it is as strong and as real as any human relationship, and just as enduring.

In July of 2001, my dog Sid passed away. She had been my loving, tail-waging companion for over 16 years. A lot of people had come and gone in my life during that time, but Sid was always there. Holding her in my arms for the last time was one of the most painful moments in my life, and yet, somehow I knew she would always be with me.

Over the past few years I have heard many stories about the lingering spirits of dogs, cats, horses and even a pig. Sometimes it seems as if the ghostly dogs and cats still wander the halls looking for their master, and sometimes the owner and pet appear together. Occasionally, the possible origin of the ghost animals can be traced, but most often they are simply another piece of the mysterious puzzle of the inexplicable. However, the following story is one of the most documented and best examples of the spirit of a beloved animal staying with his human companion long after death separated them in this world.

It's Amy Sampson's job to get the facts straight. As a reporter for the Orange County *Times Herald Record*, it's important for her to be objective, observant and capable of communicating a story. I first met Amy in the fall of 2000, when she wrote an article for the newspaper on my ghost investigation of the Peach Grove Inn in Warwick, NY. That day she mentioned a story about a poodle she had when she was a child, of how she had a terrifying premonition of the dog's death, and how she and several other people continued to see the dog years after she had died.

When I lost Sid, I was reminded of Amy's dog and asked her to share her story for this book. The following account is in her own words:

Animals have always been my best friends. I have always felt like there is no deeper connection someone can make than to an animal that is receptive to your communication. Growing up at Mount Peter Ski Area in Warwick, I had many friends in the winter, but in the summer, I had no "neighborhood" to play in. So I learned very quickly that dogs, and cats, and even the llamas down the street, could be just as good of a friend—if not better—than their human counterparts.

When I was about 6 years old, all I wanted was a poodle. I talked about it all the time and was probably relentless with my parents. For Christmas that

165

year, as I opened my presents, I was sure I was getting my wish. First I got a dog brush, then a dog bed, and then...a stuffed poodle named Princess. "You asked for a 'toy' poodle. All that stuff is for next year when you get a real dog," my mom said. I sat on the floor by the Christmas tree with my eyes fixed on the presents, trying not to cry. My dad went up to get something out of the other room, and when he opened the door, the most beautiful white poodle ran out of the room and right into my arms! I named her "Angel," and she never left my side.

Some time later, I'd say about a year, I had a scary dream. Princess, the stuffed poodle I got before my Angel, came to me and began to talk. She said, "Did you know that Angel died?" My answer was no. I already began to feel numb, the way you do when someone dies. "Follow me," she said, and led me outside the house and down the path where we kept our horses at the time.

She brought me to our horse, "Gypsy," and told me to be careful. I woke up spooked, but didn't think much more about it. A few weeks later, after coming home from a weekend away with my parents, I was hit with the bad news. My aunt was watching Angel. They were riding the horse, and in an instant that no one could ever take back, my Angel was kicked by the horse and killed.

I remember sitting on the washing machine crying right after I found out, and feeling sick to my stomach, because I should have known. Princess told me, and it came true. I didn't want to go upstairs because my Angel wasn't there. My Angel wasn't there, and that stuffed dog was. The stuffed dog that I hated—and feared. The one that still stands on top of my dresser, unable to be taken down because it's 25-year-old owner is still afraid of it.

When I was younger I had the bad habit of trying to replace one pet with another. I had a black cat named Abigail who ran away, and I immediately found another black cat, named her Abigail, and moved right on with life. So after what I still remember as a terribly long grieving period, and after looking for months and months for another poodle that I felt an instant bond with, I chose a tiny apricot-colored poodle, and named her Angel, who I quickly fell in love with, and formed a very deep bond with.

And that's when the dreams began again. In every dream, there would be both Angels following me around. They also both spoke to me. They never said anything bad, but I was always scared.

But the dreams were not all. The first time I saw my first Angel after she died, I was about 9 years old, and both my sister and I had our beds in the living room because our bedrooms were being worked on. My parents were away, and my Aunt Debbie was watching us. My sister, Rebecca, who was 11, and my aunt were watching TV, and I was lying on my bed. It was dark out and very late. I was staring into the glass of the French doors for lack of anything better to look at, when I saw my Angel sitting on the floor in the room beyond the doors. "Angel?" I called. Angel number two picked her head up from where she was lying near my stomach. I thought to myself, if my Angel is here, then what ...

"Hey, Debbie," I called softly, my voice trembling, "get over here." Debbie came to my bed, followed by Rebecca. I had them lie down, and look through the glass. They both saw her, and within minutes, the three of us—all with tears in our astonished eyes—moved our blankets to the living room floor where we camped out for the night.

"We were so scared," Debbie said, remembering very clearly what happened that night. "Then we called Uncle Roy (my uncle who lived next door at the time) and told him we just saw Angel's ghost. Of course, she was gone by then so he didn't see her, and he thought we were all crazy, but all three of us all saw her."

When I think of it now, I can still remember that moment exactly, and still to this day when I walk by those double French doors, I look to see if she is there—sitting at the far right corner, looking out at me, either out of jealousy of my other Angel, or to look out for me.

That was the last time for years that I knew for sure that I saw my first Angel after she died. There were times that I thought I saw her, but by the time I closed my eyes and re-opened them to look, she was gone. The dreams didn't stop, and I found myself sometimes looking over my shoulder even during the day.

Then, years later, I saw her again. I was 16 and with my best-human-friend:

(The following paragraph was written by my friend, Mike Donnelly, now a member of the United States Coast Guard.)

It was approximately 9 p.m. It was in the summertime and it was dark. I was 17. I initially saw Angel #1 when I was walking up the outside steps to pick up Amy. Angel looked at me as I knocked on the door. Amy came out and we walked down the steps and onto the front yard. When we got to my car I said, "Aren't you going to let Angel in?" Her face turned white and she replied, "Huh?" I repeated my question pointing to the little white poodle looking at us. Amy said very softly, "Mike, Angel is upstate with my parents." The lump in my throat dropped to my feet. (I'd always known about Angel #1, but only met Angel #2.) I've never driven so fast. When we returned, the dog was gone and so was my non-belief in ghosts.

A few months later, I was in the attic going through some old boxes when I came across a charm-necklace I had made for my first Angel. I started to cry, and told her I was so sorry I replaced her, and that I still loved her. I then went to her grave, which is at the base of Mount Peter near the big rock (anyone who has ever been there will know which one I am talking about), and tried again to say good-bye.

While I still look for her on the bottom right side of the French doors, I have not had one dream since that day. But I do know that just as my second Angel does, my first Angel loved me. Maybe that was why she let us see her, so I knew she was still there.

The French doors where Angel (#1) was seen.

Amy as a child with her beloved poodle Angel.
Photos courtesy of Amy Sampson

POOR SOULS

Patriots were marching down Willow Grove Road in Stony Point. They knew there were Redcoats in the area, but they didn't know where, and they didn't know how many.

Two British soldiers kept watch for American rebels from the windows of a small house on Willow Grove Road. They knew the rebels were in the area, and it was their job to find out where and how many. After hours of tension, waiting and listening for any sign of enemy activity, they heard sounds and then saw a sight that made their hearts sink. The Americans were coming, far more then they had expected. Far more than they could handle. There would be nowhere to run, nowhere to hide.

The Americans attacked the Redcoats inside the house and the two men fought for their lives. They lost.

Two hundred years later, these same Redcoats still walk the halls of that old house on Willow Grove Road where they lost their lives from the hot lead of muskets and the cold steel of bayonets.

The Poor House. Photo courtesy of John Scott.

The Poor House, as it is known today, has many stories to tell. In fact, it has two sets of stories, as it used to be two separate houses. While the structure made partially of bricks has stood on that spot since Revolutionary War times, the clapboard section comprising the eastern part of the house was originally built in 1765 on the other side of the street. Known as the Smith Farm House, the structure was saved from demolition in 1969 and moved next to the Poor House and connected by a ten-foot addition.

While the name of Smith is common, in this case it should be familiar to both historians and those interested in local ghosts. The original owner, Thomas Smith, was a patriot for the cause of American freedom, but he had a brother who remained a loyalist and became embroiled in one of the most infamous incidents in this country's history. That brother, Joshua Hett Smith, lived in the house where Benedict Arnold met Major Andre to turn over the plans to the fortifications at West Point. Had the plot been successful, we all might be singing "God Save the Queen" at the start of every baseball game.

Of course, the plot was discovered, Arnold escaped and Andre was hung, and both men's ghosts probably hold the record for appearances in different locations over the last 200 years. While Arnold and André are usually just seen strolling about, there may have also been a more sinister ghost created in the plot—that of a young women co-conspirator who was murdered, and still seeks vengeance on the living (see page 67).

Thomas Smith does not seem to have led the life of intrigue that his brother did, but he was a very successful landowner and left his own mark in the area in the form of houses and tracts of land. After Smith passed away, his property went through a series of owners and was used in some rather unique ways. As an obvious example, the original Poor House got its name when it was used for a time as a county alms house.

There was another unusual use for the old house—as a jail. The house was very small when first constructed, but over the centuries it underwent many alterations and additions (including an entire house). One of those additions was a small oval room on the north side. According to the late historian Dan deNoyelles, a pair of old leg irons was found in the dirt floor of this room when it was excavated to pour a concrete floor. There are stories that the jail room was used to hold prisoners awaiting trial and sentencing from the local circuit-riding judge who traveled among his jurisdictions.

I first became aware of the Poor House hauntings when someone told me that her best friend used to live in the house and they would hear chains rattling in the jail cell and the sounds of moaning and heavy footsteps throughout the house. She added that, "Everyone who grew up around there knew about the ghosts at the Poor House." While it's always nice to have everybody know about it, I do try to get a little more substantial evidence. Unfortunately, I made several attempts to contact the owners at the time, but did not receive any response.

The ghosts that have been documented are those of the two British soldiers. One of the owners in the 1940s was a set designer who worked in New York City. One night he had to stay in the city, leaving his male houseguest alone. Although he had not mentioned a word about the legend of the hauntings, when he returned the next day, the guest was visibly pale and trembling. Naturally curious as to his friend's terrified countenance, he asked what had happened.

His friend claimed that he was relaxing by the pool for a while and then decided to go back into the house. When he entered through the kitchen door, he could see straight into the living room where a man was standing by the fireplace. Of course, this was no ordinary man—he was dressed in a red military coat and was wearing boots and all of the other accoutrements of "a British soldier or something." He was probably right on both accounts; the man was once a British soldier, but now was something else—something like a ghost.

On another occasion, an owner was having a large dinner party. One of his female guests did not believe that he was the actual owner, and it took some persuading to convince her. When asked why she didn't believe he owned the house, she replied that she had met a man in a red coat who claimed that this house was *his house*. Too bad she hadn't asked his name, rank and serial number.

Another owner of the original Poor House in the 1940s, a Lucky Morra, proved to be not so lucky. A bar-owner in New York City, he was described as a man who had rather bizarre tastes, entertained some unusual people at the house and died young under "mysterious circumstances." Perhaps Un-Lucky Morra's spirit has also joined those of the British soldiers and the prisoners from the jail cell.

It is apparent that many interesting characters, both living and dead, have inhabited the two houses that are now one. Generations of people have claimed to see, hear and feel strange things there. However, there have been some occupants who have not experienced anything unusual, but that could be accounted for in several ways. The occupants may not have been sensitive or were in complete denial, or the spirits may have chosen to be quiet for a while.

Skeptics would say that there is another choice, that there is no basis in fact for these stories and that all of these people have imagined the figures and sounds. However, that excuse just doesn't seem to add up. How can so many different people over such a long period of time have experienced identical things, even though they had no previous knowledge of the place?

No, the only thing that does add up is that one haunted house plus another haunted house does indeed equal one big haunted house.

THE VANISHING GHOST TOWN

When I conducted the investigation at the Peach Grove Inn in Warwick for the K104.7 radio broadcast in November, 2000, Andre (the producer) told me about a haunted ghost town in Wawarsing. Legend had it that long ago a man there killed his entire family and then hung himself. The town was eventually abandoned, but spirits still lingered and terrorized those brave, or foolish, enough to venture back into the deep, dark woods. It sounded like a perfect spot.

Bob and I went to investigate the alleged ghost town with only this information. Had nothing happened that night, I wouldn't have pursued it further. However, what did happen convinced me to find out as much as I could about Lundy Road and its inhabitants, past and present.

After that eventful night, I contacted some local historians, and while nobody was able to confirm the murder/suicide story, they did provide some information about the abandoned town at the end of the present-day Lundy Road. That town, Pottersville, began in the 1850s when Francis Potter built a sawmill, and homes for the workers soon sprang up around it. The mill burned in 1870 and the Potters moved away, as did most of the workers and their families.

Pottersville was occupied again early in the 20th century, but a flood in 1928 caused the town to be abandoned for the second time. In the 1930s,

Frederick Lundy purchased the town and eventually bought thousands of acres surrounding it. Lundy was famous for his Lundy's seafood restaurant in Sheepshead Bay, Brooklyn, which claimed to be the largest restaurant in the country with seating for 2,800.

Lundy was an eccentric recluse, which was possibly the result of a history of personal tragedies. Both of his parents and three of his brothers died before he was 25. Two of his business associates were shot and he was robbed and actually kidnapped on one occasion. He did not want strangers near his property and women were never allowed in the mansion he built on Lundy Road. Guests slept in cabins or tents.

In his last years, Lundy (who came to be called the Howard Hughes of New York) lived in rooms over his restaurant where his paranoia caused him to order that all of the windows be painted over so no one could see in. He died in 1977.

Today, the Lundy property is in new hands and the mansion is being restored. However, 5,400 acres of the land is now the property of New York State and will be protected open space. While this is a boon to conservationists, it signaled the death of the ghost town.

When Bob and I first went to find the ghost town one winter's night, the only information I had was that there was at least one haunted house way back in the woods. We turned onto Lundy Road and the cluster of modern houses there did not prepare us for what lay ahead. A short distance in, thick woods came right up to the road's edge and the van's headlights only managed to cut a narrow tunnel in the darkness.

After about a quarter of a mile we were sure the town had to be just up ahead. Half a mile in we wondered if we had the right road. We drove further and further into the heavily wooded blackness and finally the headlights caught the edges of a stone wall. Stopping the van, we saw that there was a beautiful 18th century-style stone house facing away from the road. We got out and stood in the enshrouding darkness and silence, feeling very much like we were firmly in the middle of nowhere.

That feeling was enhanced by the fact that with all the bags of equipment we brought, we had forgotten to bring a single flashlight! Fortunately, we had the infrared camera and the night vision scope that has a high-powered infrared light. Letting our equipment see for us, we walked along the two sides facing the road. High grass and uneven ground kept us from going around to the front of the house. (Normally, I would have attempted it, but while a twisted ankle is one thing, a twisted camcorder is not acceptable.)

We took quite a few pictures with the 35mm cameras and a conventional flash, and in the brief bursts of light we could see that every door and window was securely boarded up. It was clear that they didn't want anyone to get in. Too bad they didn't think about something that might want to come out.

After about ten minutes, we decided there wasn't much else to see, and as absolutely nothing seemed out of the ordinary, we started packing up to leave. I was quite disappointed that after all the hype, nothing happened. This was the first time I used my new infrared camera and not a single drop of spirit energy had appeared. No lights, no sounds, no nothing.

My stubbornness kicked in and I decided that I was going to take the camcorder and go into the grass and weeds after all. Maybe the ghosts were all in the front of the house? (Yes, I admit that sounded just as irrational then as it does now.) I continued taping in Nightshot as I started along the side of the house, and just happened to aim the camcorder toward the boarded up door I had previously photographed. I stopped dead in my tracks.

I was not looking at a closed door anymore. Suddenly, I was looking straight into the house through an open doorway! The infrared pierced the darkness and revealed the rooms on the interior of the house. For a moment, it actually felt like the old house was beckoning me to come inside and I took a few steps forward. As I was being drawn toward the house, I remembered that a minute earlier that open door was closed. It was very quiet there, there was no wind, and neither of us had heard the door open. Something was not right.

"Bob?" I called out. "Wasn't this door closed?"

He replied that as far as he knew the entire house was nailed shut.

I taped for another few seconds and started to back away. Pulling out my 35mm camera, I took another picture. As much as I felt compelled to enter the house, there was a sense of danger, as well. I didn't know if the house was structurally safe. I didn't know what living people might have been using the house for shelter, or other more sinister purposes. And I still didn't know how a door that was nailed shut had silently opened on a house rumored to be haunted by a malevolent spirit. It was time to leave.

When we got home, I immediately connected the camcorder to the television so we could view the interior of the house and try to solve the mystery of the opening door. The footage of the exterior of the house came out fine, but when the tape came to the section where I was looking into the interior of the house, there was nothing there. It was as if the camera had chosen to stop recording. There was blank tape, and then suddenly the recording began again once I left the open doorway and came back to the van. My crucial camcorder evidence was nonexistent. I would have to wait for the 35mm film to be developed.

A couple of days passed before I went to pick up the pictures. As I stood in the store, I immediately flipped through the photos and came across the one I took when we first arrived. The door was solid and closed tight. Then I pulled out the last photo I took. Forgetting where I was, I expressed my shock out loud in words I normally do not use in public.

There was the open doorway, but even more bizarre was that only *part* of the door was open, and *part* of the board above the transom was missing! There is no sign that these sections swung forward or back, they had simply vanished!

In the days after our visit, I tried to make sense of what I had seen, that somehow a breeze we hadn't felt, or perhaps a squatter we didn't see, had managed to silently open that door while we were standing there. Now, however, as I looked at the pictures of the partially missing door and the piece above it, I had no explanation.

Winter snows soon set in, and we didn't return to Lundy Road until spring. I had learned since our first visit that we hadn't even come close to Pottersville, that the main body of the ghost town was miles past the stone house. While I couldn't imagine anything more remote, we were determined to find the other houses, and this time we were going in daylight. We had also learned that as part of the deal for the land to become protected space, the houses of the ghost town were going to be demolished. The clock was ticking.

As we approached the stone house, we saw many other structures, both mostly intact and completely ruined, that we hadn't seen in the darkness of our first trip. The stone house itself had been recently boarded up again, this time with new plywood covering every door and window, so I was unable to examine the mysterious doorway.

We continued past the stone house and were amazed at just how many miles this road stretched. We finally came to the gates of Lundy's mansion, and saw that tarps covered the roof and that the renovations were underway. The road became extremely rough past this point and neither of us relished the thought of breaking down miles from anywhere.

The road branched at one point and we turned down a tree-lined lane and found several modest houses and a barn. Getting back to the "main" road, we were determined to make Pottersville or bust. Unfortunately, the narrow, rocky road became so bad that when we came to a section with a recent wash-out, we realized that continuing in a van with low clearance was foolish. So close, yet so far.

On the way back, we met a few people in a Jeep about to attempt the bad part of the road and stopped to talk to them. The driver had lived in the area his entire life, and when I asked if he knew anything about Lundy Road (I didn't mention a word about ghosts), his immediate reaction was, "Weird **** goes on back here!" (By shear coincidence, he happened to use the same word I had in the store when I saw the photos!) He related some stories he and his parents had heard—stories stretching back to the time before the European settlers arrived. While this was hardly rock-solid evidence, it did add to the lore and legend of the place. Apparently the area was considered haunted for at least a few hundred years.

Soon after our second visit, I e-mailed Mike Worden and suggested that I had the perfect terrain for him to try out his new Jeep. We arranged to meet one summer's evening, but that afternoon he was called into work. (Mike is a police officer in Port Jervis.) Heavy rain cancelled our next attempt. Finally, on the last Saturday in August of 2001, Bob and I met Mike and Autumn at the end of Lundy Road. It was 6 pm, with plenty of daylight left, until we hit the heavily wooded area where darkness already started to fill the forest.

We were pleased to find the stone house still standing, but surprised to find that all of the doors and windows were now sealed with cinderblocks. As Mike commented, "They are either trying really hard to keep people out, or keep something in!"

Continuing on past Lundy's mansion, we parked the van and got into Mike's Jeep. It was rough going as we bounced our way deeper and deeper into the woods. We turned off at the branch in the road Bob and I had found and discovered the houses were now all gone except for their chimneys. A couple from New Jersey was poking through the rubble and they volunteered that they were not there for relics—they were looking for the ghosts. "Everybody knows there's ghosts back here. A lot of weird **** goes on," they said. I guess "everybody" can't be wrong!

Back on the road to Pottersville, I joked that we must be getting close to the Canadian border. Finally, we found the ghost town—or what was left of it. The houses had been knocked down, burned and plowed over. It had happened so recently that one site was still smoldering, with a single column of smoke rising out of the ruins.

One of my favorite expressions is that timing is everything. Unfortunately, our timing was off. By just a matter of days, we missed the houses that had stood for generations. We were not happy campers.

Still, we scanned the fresh ruins with the EMF meter, but found nothing. Curiously, however, both Autumn and I took some pictures with our automatic 35mm cameras and found that they were acting "slow." When you pressed the shutter release there was a substantial lag before the camera snapped the pictures. They both worked fine before we got there, and worked fine again after we left Pottersville.

The road continued past the ruins and we walked along it for a while. However, we had no idea how much further it went and it was beginning to get seriously dark. It was also clearly dinnertime for the local bug population. Swarms of insects soon surrounded us.

Although I was disappointed that the ghost town had vanished, I have seen enough to know that if there are spirits along the length of Lundy Road, a few bulldozers can't drive them out. Generations of the local population have grown up with stories and legends of hauntings there and as hikers begin to pass through this new state land, I'm sure a few new stories will be added.

The only solid evidence I was able to gather was the decidedly un-solid door of the stone house. Of all the things I have seen and heard and felt during my investigations, this one has made one of the greatest impressions on me. I don't know why, but even today as I recall standing in the silent darkness, looking through the camcorder straight into that house, a shudder runs up my spine.

Did murders and suicides take place at one time in the houses along Lundy Road? With so many hundreds of years of history, anything is possible. Wherever mankind has lived, loved, hated and died, spirits may linger.

Put on your hiking boots, grab a flashlight, hop in your favorite 4-wheel drive vehicle and take a trip down Lundy Road. Perhaps the remaining stone chimneys will lead you to sites of tragedies long forgotten, and as night falls fast and hard, the deep, dark woods may reveal some of their mysteries.

***

In November of 2001, the local newspaper reported that a man had been killed in the woods of Lundy Road. A hunter was charged with criminally negligent homicide for shooting another hunter in the head with a rifle. No other details of the incident were released.

One cannot help but wonder if this latest tragedy will add another haunting to the vanishing ghost town.

The photo of the closed door (left) taken soon after we arrived. Note that the door and portion above the transom are solid wood and securely closed.

The last photo (right) I took showing the inside of the house through the open doorway. Note that only part of the wood door is open, as is part of the area above the transom. It is not as if the door was just opened, it is simply gone!

THE MOST HAUNTED HOUSE I
NEW JERSEY

I know this is a book about hauntings in the Hudson Valley, and Sussex County, New Jersey is not in the boundaries of the Hudson Valley. However, if you don't mind a little detour to the western part of that state, I think the following story will be worth your time. After all, it is about the most haunted house in New Jersey.

By the time Thomas Hunt built a house along the Bear Creek in Sussex County, New Jersey in 1835, the area already had homes, mills and distilleries that were over 50 years old. As generations passed, the Hunt house went through many hands and even served as an inn and a stagecoach stop. By the time Glenn and Jackie Wershing purchased the property in 1961, the house had a long and colorful history. However, those colors seemed to be primarily shades of gray and white—the color of ghosts.

The Wershing house.

"We knew something strange was going on here right after we moved in," said Glenn. "Again and again we would hear footsteps on the third floor running from the back of the house to the front. When the footsteps stopped there would be a big 'thump' as if something was hitting the floor or wall. I would grab a flashlight and run upstairs to see what was going on the never found anything. We must have heard those footsteps and that thumping sound 100 times and each time I would run up there and find nothing."

The Wershing's three children were terrified by the phantom footsteps, but the sounds weren't confined to the third floor. Often, the distinct sound of steps would come down from that floor and stop right in front of the Wershing's daughters' second floor bedroom. This is not to say that they were heard coming down the stairs and across the hall. No, these footsteps came right down the wall, and in Glenn's words they, "scared my daughters half to death!"

Jackie and Glenn Wershing

The girls' bedroom window opened to a section of the roof and on many nights terrifying noises drove the girls out of the window. They would then climb down to the ground and run to a neighbor's house to sleep.

Their son was not immune to the goings on, either. While many areas of the house suddenly grew cold, signifying that "they" were there, one incident in particular made the son also run from the house in the middle of the night. An icy wind suddenly filled his third-floor bedroom and held him down against the bed. He was unable to move and "all sorts of wild things" began filling his mind. Before this possession could be completed, however, he used every ounce of his strength and managed to throw himself off the bed. He got up, ran out of the house and spent the night with a friend.

The footsteps, strange sounds, and cold spots became an almost daily occurrence on the third floor. Even the family dogs would not climb the stairs unless urged to do so, and even then they were uncomfortable and agitated for as long as they were up there.

However, these occurrences on the third floor are only the tip of the paranormal iceberg in the Wershing house. One of the most frequent manifestations is that of the "balls of light." The first time one made an appearance was in the middle of the night at the foot of one of the girl's beds. Waking up, she saw a dull, white light, about the size of the basketball, hanging over her bed and she began to scream. Glenn ran into her room and cautiously approached the light. It floated slowly around the bed and stopped. As he tried to approach it again, it went out the door, across the hall and into his son's bedroom where it disappeared.

"I was worried," Glenn said, "because I didn't know if it was ball lightning, or St. Elmo's Fire...or a ghost."

These balls or orbs of light are seen predominantly in the second floor bedrooms and around the fireplace in a living room on that floor. Jackie inspected the fireplace to see if whether these things could be entering the house through the chimney, but she found that the fireplace was completely sealed off and nothing could come in that way—at least nothing normal.

Naturally curious as to what might be behind the bizarre encounters, the Wershings began to question neighbors and former residents. The story came out that during the 1930s when the house was being rented to local workers, it was difficult to keep tenants for any length of time. The problem was not with the rent or accommodations, it was the frequent orbs of light that terrified the grown men living there and sent them scurrying for less "active" places to live.

Other information from a neighbor helped shed light on another series of bizarre occurrences. If you ever have a chance to look through the Wershing family photo album, you may be puzzled by the occasional picture of four children. Recalling that the Wershing's only had three children, one might assume the extra boy was a relative or friend. But if you look closely at those pictures, the fourth child always appears hazy and indistinct. That would be because when those photos were taken, there were only three living, breathing children there.

A psychic who once visited the house entered through the side kitchen entrance and immediately said, "You know you have the spirit of a young boy here. He used to play here when he was alive and now spends a lot of time in the house and yard. He is usually waiting right outside this door."

Jackie and Glenn decided to once more ask the neighbors and former residents if they had any information about a young boy who may have played at the house. Their elderly neighbor just up the street said that in the 1930s, the local boys would use the steep road for sledding. His 9-year-old son was sledding with them one day when he careened into a large tree that stood on the Wershing's property right by the side door. He was killed instantly. Perhaps it is this boy's spirit that waits by the door and sometimes comes into the house to join in the family photos, trying to recapture some of the life cut so short.

There may be other clues as to the nature of the many spirits in the house. Glenn is an avid archaeologist and historian, and one day he unearthed an ancient Indian skull nearby. (The area has yielded numerous artifacts of early

Indian settlements.) Against Jackie's misgivings, he decided it would be fun to put the skull in the center of the candy tray for Halloween. The kids were to come in the kitchen door, and if they were brave enough, take the candy from the skull tray.

Glenn put the tray in the center of the table and they went into an adjoining room to wait for the little trick or treaters. However, only moments after leaving the kitchen, they heard a terrible crashing sound. Rushing back in, they found the skull in the center of the floor, smashed into a hundred pieces. The tray of candy was untouched. If the skull had somehow managed to simply roll off the table, it wouldn't have ended up smashed in the center of the room, it would have broken where it fell.

Are there also Indian spirits in the Wershing house—spirits who were angered by the use of a skull for a Halloween prop?

Yet another incident may or may not be related to the ghosts, but it certainly qualifies as bizarre. When the Wershing's granddaughter was a child, she was the Queen of the Sussex Farm and Horse Show. The young queen's reign was commemorated by a doll that was made to look like her. The Wershings kept the doll on a table in the first floor living room and one day many years later Jackie found the doll on the floor. She couldn't understand how the doll would suddenly fall after standing there for such a long time, but she was used to the unexplainable and simply placed the doll back on the table.

At the time, their granddaughter was attending college in New Mexico. One of the buildings on campus was undergoing renovations to remove asbestos. In order to keep the asbestos contained, the building was sealed and kept under negative pressure, although they did not post warning signs. As their granddaughter was entering the building, the heavy door slammed shut and caught her right hand, severing the tip of her index finger.

Soon after hearing the news of the freak accident, Jackie took a closer look at the doll that had fallen, and was stunned to see that the tip of the doll's right index finger was missing! The injury to their granddaughter was mirrored exactly in her doll. No one is sure which event occurred first that day, but it might be a good idea to put the doll in a very safe place where it cannot fall or sustain any further damage!

The doll with the severed finger.

As of yet, I have not mentioned a "traditional" ghost sighting, but this, too, has occurred in the Wershing house. In the faint light of early dawn, Jackie turned over in her bed and saw an old woman standing in her room. The woman was short, dressed in an old-fashioned white nightgown and had very long hair. While the woman was only in shades of gray and white, she was solid and three-dimensional, and she stood in front of the only mirror in the room, seemingly looking at herself.

Jackie tried to remain very still and quiet, but she wanted to see the woman's face, in hopes of being able to identify her in the photos of former residents. Moving slowly, Jackie leaned over to catch a glimpse of the woman's reflection in the mirror. There was none. If this ghost had a face, it was incapable of being seen in a mirror. A few moments later the old woman simply vanished.

Unfortunately, not all the paranormal activity in the house is so benign. In addition to the incident with her son, there have been three additional attacks, all of which happened to Jackie, and each one occurring when Glenn was away on business.

The first time, Jackie was awakened by a blast of bitter cold air. The pressure in the room felt so high she couldn't get out of bed—something, or someone, was holding her down. She screamed, but her children didn't hear any sounds. This phantom attacker was apparently capable of also stifling her cries. The pressure and terror grew, until she fainted.

When Jackie came to around 5am, the cold and pressure were gone, but something very tangible remained. There were red marks and bruises on her legs and ankles, as if something very powerful had held her down. That morning she asked the children if they had heard any sounds in the night, but they hadn't and she didn't want to frighten them (any more than they already were by the strange sights and sounds in that house) by relating the details of the attack.

Unfortunately, it was to happen again, and the details of this encounter are perhaps the most frightening of all. Glenn was away on business and Jackie was alone in bed, sleeping on her side. Something woke her up and in addition to the icy air, she felt a physical form pressing against her from behind.

"I could feel its heartbeat behind me, leaning up against me. I could also hear and feel it breathing."

Finding the courage to reach back, her hand touched something solid with hair like a dog or some other kind of animal.

"Then it started to try to talk through me, through my mouth. It was making a guttural voice way in the back of my throat. That scared the hell out of me!"

Running out of the room, she stayed up the rest of the night until it was time to go to work. Whatever this thing was, it was now personal; it was now

181

trying to use Jackie's body to speak. She confesses that this was the most terrifying of all the incidents she had experienced in the house. However, the incident that occurred later that same week was a close second.

The Wershing's daughter was away at college at the time, so Jackie thought that she could avoid the creature trying to use her body by sleeping in her daughter's room. Unfortunately, in the Wershing house you can run, but you can not hide. And if you do try to run, you apparently only make the spirits angrier.

As she slept in her daughter's bed, yet another blast of icy cold air awoke her. This time the moment she opened her eyes some powerful force struck her in the side. The impact was so severe it flipped her over. Stunned and in pain, Jackie struggled to get out of bed and as she stood up her blood ran cold as an ominous voice declared, "Found yooooouuu!"

"It spoke the words very slowly and it was letting me know that even though I changed rooms it could still find me. I wouldn't sleep in that house alone again, and stayed with my other daughter the rest of the week until Glenn came home."

Was this hairy, violent spirit the ghost of an animal, or something more sinister, something demonic? A psychic who visited the house claimed to

Jackie's bed, where an attack occurred.

have encountered a beast-like demon in Glenn's study. His study contains some ancient Indian artifacts and the psychic felt that the demon was brought into the house through them. An exorcism was performed, and perhaps it was successful as no further attacks occurred. However, not all the paranormal activity ceased. Orbs of light still wander through the house on a regular basis, phantom footsteps, slamming doors and other inexplicable sounds can still be heard, objects move on their own and the presence of spirits is evident in many other ways. Teams of psychics have visited the Wershing house and it has been featured on several television shows, including *Sightings*.

I first became aware of the house in December of 2000, when I received an e-mail from Orlando Rodriguez. Orlando was putting together a film on haunted places and had already been to the Wershing house. Several strange things occurred during his visit, including capturing on tape a small glass figurine spinning around on a table and then flying onto the floor and smashing. No one was within six feet of the figurine at the time it decided to move on its own.

We arranged to visit the Wershing house in January of 2001, and Bob and I packed up our equipment and looked forward to our investigation. Glenn and Jackie were very gracious and accommodating hosts, and they immediately struck me as intelligent, articulate, good natured and quite credible. Despite all that has occurred in the last forty years, there is still some healthy skepticism, and they are not ready to cry "Ghost!" at everything that goes bump in the night.

With cameras, tape recorders and meters running, we started our tour of the house. Nothing seemed to be out of the ordinary on the first floor. However, as I climbed the staircase, the EMF meter started registering high readings on the top few steps, and my own internal "meters" went off, as well. I always try to approach these investigations as scientifically and rationally as possible, but we all possess psychic ability and some places make it very difficult to ignore those abilities. Among other things, I got the distinct impression that in the Wershing house it was intuition, not instruments, that would be the best gauge.

In fact, as we were to later discover, for some reason the camcorder malfunctioned and over an hour of taping yielded just a few minutes of tape (although just those few minutes showed some of those tiny lights flitting around in infrared that we have seen in other places). Also, one of the 35mm cameras refused to work, even though it had worked before arriving and it worked again after we left. As I examined the camera, trying to figure out why it would not take pictures when everything indicated that it was functioning, the Wershings told me that malfunctioning equipment is nothing new in that house.

Arrows point to the light, hazy patch that appeared in the "negative" room on the third floor.

At least my internal sensors were working and they kicked into high gear on the third floor. In a room to the right of the staircase (once a bedroom now used for storage), I was flooded with negative feelings—hostility, anger, fear, aggression—and those negative forces seemed directed across the hall. One of our photographs in that room revealed a large white, hazy area stretching from the center of the room to ceiling, although we didn't see anything at the time. Leaving that room rather quickly (it was decidedly uncomfortable) I crossed the hall and went into another former bedroom, now also used for storage. The difference was like night and day.

While that room felt more comforting and positive, it was still unnerving. (That may not appear to make sense, but trust me, when you're standing in a haunted house, especially one with a whole host of ghosts, your emotional scale can be played from one end to the other, and all at the same time.) My overall impression (and it was a *very* strong impression) was that there were powerful positive and negative forces in the house, constantly pushing back and forth. I hate to sound melodramatic, but as long as I am wading in psychic waters I might as well shoot the works; it felt like a battleground of good against evil.

I explained to everyone what I was feeling, how this appeared to be a house divided, a house where one half was in constant struggle with the other half. Fully expecting at least some snickering at the suggestion, Jackie instead looked thoughtful and replied, "You know several psychics have said that. They say that this part of the house (Jackie pointed to what I perceived to be the negative part) is where the evil forces are and this part (pointing to the "good" half) is where the good or positive energies are." It was comforting to know that if I was hallucinating, at least I wasn't alone.

Glenn had some fascinating information about the physical construction of the house, which may help explain some of the psychical phenomena. It was built right on top of a geological fault line—a place where the Earth itself is in a constant struggle between opposing forces.

Strange lights have been reported along fault lines around the world. In fact, some scientists suggest that an increase in light activity may signal an approaching earthquake. While these types of lights may be purely the result of natural disturbances as rock is squeezed under enormous pressures, there could also be other consequences as in the case of the Wershing's wandering orbs. Just as deep wells and natural springs can be magnets for paranormal energies, perhaps fault lines also attract forces we have yet to understand.

Glenn also said that the actual foundation support is in the form of just one massive beam running down the middle of the house. This one beam acts as a type of see-saw, and the house can actually shift from side to side, ever so slightly, but noticeably. If ever a house was a study in balance, this is it.

When I was in the "positive" bedroom on the third floor, I was walking slowly around with the EMF meter as Bob and Orlando stood by the door. Suddenly, it felt like something light and wispy brushed across the center of my forehead. Orlando has me on tape (at least his camera was working!) swatting at what I assumed to be cobwebs. I couldn't feel any cobwebs with my hand, nor could I see any, and the tingling sensation on my forehead continued even after I wiped and rubbed my skin several times trying to remove whatever was causing it. The tingling, wispy feeling persisted, and went deeper than just the surface of my skin. This added to the general unnerving feeling to the room and I was happy to leave it.

As I was examining another part of the house, Orlando went back to that room and closely looked at the ceilings and walls where I had been standing. He said there were absolutely no cobwebs anywhere in that room. Later, when we were all in the kitchen, the tingling in the center of my forehead occurred once more, and again, no external explanation was found. This was not a sensation I had ever before experienced, and have not experienced since, although Bob Strong and Mike Worden would later feel the "cobweb effect" in the Laurel Grove Cemetery (see page 140).

(Now I'm sure some of you readers are jumping up and down at this point saying that the center of the forehead is the location of the "third eye," or the seat of intuition. If that is truly the case and something that night was trying to get my attention, it definitely scored a direct bull's-eye!)

Despite all that happened that night, I'm sure we just scratched the surface of the paranormal activity in the Wershing house. Perhaps the unusual activity was present as far back as the time of the ancient Native American communities in the area, or perhaps Thomas Hunt just picked the wrong piece of property. It is also possible that there was a gradual accumulation of spirits over the years as people died there and generations of trials and tribulations left their psychic imprints.

Whatever is behind these numerous and varied phenomena, after forty years the Wershings have learned to live with them. They have all had more than their share of terrifying moments, and there is no guarantee that there aren't more to come, but it is a beautiful house and property, and it is their home. All things considered, both the living and the dead have learned to co-exist in the most haunted house in New Jersey.

This may look like a photo of a glowing-eyed ghost, but it's just how I look in infrared as I search for real ghosts at the Wershing house.

185

Copy this page to use for your own ghost hunt. If you know of a haunted site you think should be considered for an upcoming book, please contact me at:
P.O. Box 192, Blooming Grove, NY, 10914
www.ghostinvestigator.com

Field Report

Date: Location:

Time In: Weather:

Names of People Interviewed:

Equipment: Camera ☐ Video ☐ Tape Recorder ☐
                        Thermometer ☐   Other:

Experiences: Sounds ☐ Odors ☐ Cold Spots ☐
        Visuals ☐ Touch/Sensations ☐ Movement ☐

Details (Attach extra sheet if necessary):

Time Out: Total Time on Site:

Conclusions:

Prepared and Signed by:

Witness(es):

Printed in the United States
6384

9 780971 232600